Passport's

ME

MW00527079

SECOND EDITION

FROM
THOMAS
COOK

PASSPORT BOOKS
NTC/Contemporary Publishing Group

This edition first published in 2000 by Passport Books
A division of NTC/Contemporary Publishing Group, Inc.
4255 West Touhy Avenue,
Lincolnwood (Chicago), Illinois
60712–1975 U.S.A.

Written by Mona King

Original photography by Rick Strange and Robert Holmes

Edited, designed, and produced by AA Publishing.
© The Automobile Association 1995, 1999.
Maps © The Automobile Association 1995, 1999.

Library of Congress Catalog Card Number: 98-67243

ISBN 0-8442-1154-0

The contents of this publication are believed correct at the time of
printing. Nevertheless, the publishers cannot accept responsibility for
any errors or omissions, or for changes in the details given in this guide,
or for the consequences of any reliance on the information provided by
the same. Assessments of attractions, hotels, restaurants, and so forth are
based upon the author's own experience and therefore descriptions given
in this guide necessarily contain an element of subjective opinion which
may not reflect the publisher's opinion or dictate a reader's own
experiences on another occasion.
**We have tried to ensure accuracy in this guide, but things do
change and we would be grateful if readers would advise us of any
inaccuracies they may encounter.**

Published by Passport Books in conjunction with AA Publishing and the
Thomas Cook Group Ltd.

Color separation: BTB Colour Reproduction, Whitchurch, Hampshire,
England.

Printed by Edicoes ASA, Oporto, Portugal.

Cover Photographs: front and spine, copyright © Jan Butchofsky-
Houser/Dave G. Houser Stock Photography.

Contents

About This Book

BACKGROUND

FIRST STEPS

WHAT TO SEE

GETTING AWAY
FROM IT ALL

DIRECTORY

This book is divided into five sections,
identified by the above color coding.

Background gives an introduction to
the country – its history, geography,
politics, and culture.

First Steps offers practical advice on
arriving and getting around.
What to See is an alphabetical listing
of places to visit, interspersed with
walks and tours.
Getting Away from It All highlights
places off the beaten track where it's
possible to relax and enjoy peace and
quiet.
Finally, the **Directory** provides
practical information – from shopping
and entertainment to children and
sports, including a section on business
matters. Special highly illustrated
features on specific aspects of the
country appear throughout the book.

Local buses, like this one in Oaxaca, are used
mainly by Mexicans going about their business

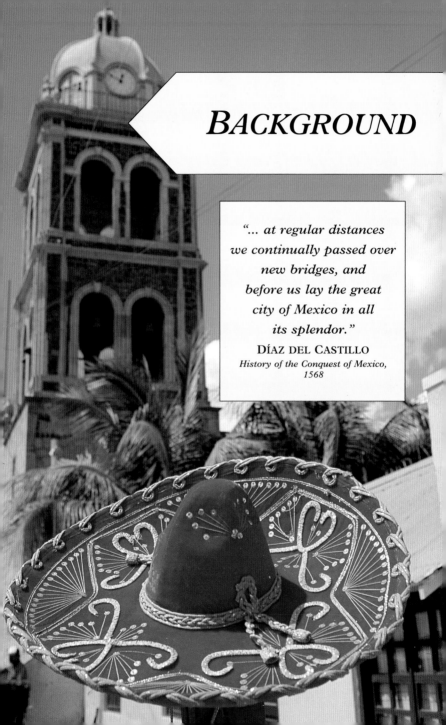

BACKGROUND

"... at regular distances we continually passed over new bridges, and before us lay the great city of Mexico in all its splendor."

DÍAZ DEL CASTILLO
*History of the Conquest of Mexico,
1568*

Introduction

Mexico's sharp contrasts of geography, climate, and culture make it a fascinating place. Coastal resorts offer sun and relaxation; pre-Columbian ruins beckon from deep in the jungle; colonial cities recall the grandeur of the Spanish Empire; national parks offer wildlife and tranquility; genteel spa resorts provide retreats in surroundings that attracted emperors centuries ago.

MEXICO

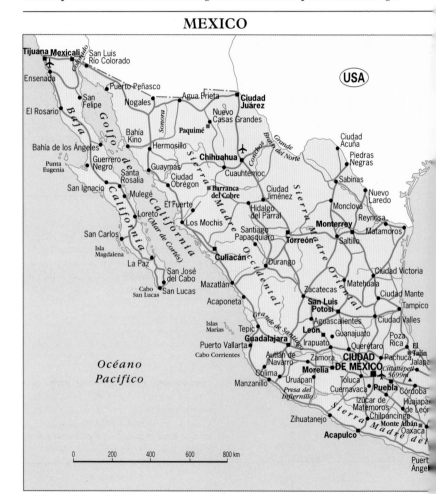

Top: view over Zapotec ruins, Monte Albán
Above: typical desert landscape

The majority of Mexicans are Spanish-speaking *mestizos*, a mixture of native Indians and Spaniards. But the country has a large indigenous population living in their ancestral lands, preserving their own language, dress, crafts, and customs. Local Indian markets and *fiestas* make for memorable experiences.

This country of contradiction is bound to have some impact on you – whatever your response, it won't be indifference. There is something about Mexico that sets it apart. It has a lot to do with the Mexicans themselves, who treat the stranger in their midst with unusual warmth. And few countries offer so much to the foreign traveler for what is still so little money. The place can work a kind of magic on you, making you want to return again and again. As the saying goes: "Once the dust of Mexico has settled on your heart, you will find peace in no other land."

Geography

Shaped rather like a horn, Mexico lies between the 14th and 32nd parallels. It shares a 3,200km border with the United States to the north, and is bounded by Guatemala and Belize to the south. With an area of 1,970,000sq km, it is about one quarter of the size of the United States.

Mexico is a country of dramatic contrasts, ranging from desert in the north to tropical jungles in the south; to the west lies 7,338km of Pacific coastline, while 2,805km of eastern shores border the Gulf of Mexico and the Caribbean Sea. Its wildly varying altitudes provide a richness and diversity of landscapes and climates. There are three main climatic zones: the *tierras calientes* (hot lands), which go from sea level up to 800m; the *tierras templadas* (temperate lands) which lie between 800m and about 1,700m above sea level; and the *tierras frías* (cold lands), which include the highest elevations.

High country

Some 60 percent of the land is covered by mountainous terrain, and great mountain ranges dominate its

landscapes. The Sierra Madre Oriental and the Sierra Madre Occidental run down the east and west of the country, respectively. These are linked by the Sistema Volcánica Transversal volcanic range, which forms a natural divide between the north and south of the country. In this area are Mexico's highest peaks and some of its loveliest: the beautiful snow-capped volcanoes of Pico de Orizaba (5,699m), Popocatépetl (5,452m), and Iztaccíhuatl (5,286m). Between the two mighty mountain ranges lies the Altiplano, or High Plateau, covering the northern and central region of Mexico. The Sierra Madre del Sur range continues along the southwest coast, terminating in the green belt of Chiapas, which borders Guatemala.

Lakes and rivers

Mexico's most attractive natural lakes are to be found in the central highlands and in the southeast. Lago de Chapala, south of Guadalajara, is the largest lake, measuring 80km by 20km. Others of interest, in neighboring Michoacán, are Lake Pátzcuaro, south of Morelia, and Lake Cuitzeo, which shrinks during the dry season. Lesser known is the volcanic lake of Catemaco, southeast of Veracruz. In southern Chiapas are the Lagunas de Monte Bello, a beautiful region of multi-

The thorny arms of cacti stretch skyward out of the scrubby terrain of Baja California

The jagged peaks of the Sierra de la Giganta, near Loreto, seem to discourage familiarity

colored lakes. The Yucatán features many lovely lagoons with crystal-clear waters.

The most famous river in Mexico is the Río Bravo (Rio Grande in the United States), which forms a large part of the border with the United States as it flows into the Gulf of Mexico. The Sonora, Yaqui, and Fuerte rivers irrigate the arid north and flow into the Gulf of California. The central region is served mainly by the rivers Balsa, Lerma, and Moctezuma. In the southeast are the rivers Grijalva and Usumacinta (which rises in Guatemala), which empty their waters into the Bahía de Campeche (Bay of Campeche). A number of dams (*presas*) built in various parts of the country provide irrigation and electricity.

Rainfall

The central regions of Mexico have a well-defined rainy season, which falls roughly between late May and early October. Rainfall is minimal in northern Mexico and Baja California, while the rain forests of southeastern Mexico are subject to much more frequent rain year round. But, as in the rest of the world, weather patterns in Mexico seem to be increasingly less predictable, with uncharacteristic spells suddenly making an appearance. In general, the best time to visit is from November to May.

Flora and Fauna

*W*ith its varying altitudes and different climatic zones, Mexico is blessed with a wealth of plant and animal life, both native and introduced over the centuries. Thousands of varieties of flowers, shrubs, and trees surround you, adorning streets, courtyards, and gardens. Traveling farther afield, you can enjoy a fantastic diversity of wildlife.

Tropical blossom and trees

Wherever you go in Mexico, you cannot escape the vibrant colors of nature. Widely seen are the many hues of bougainvillaea, hibiscus, gold cup, frangipani, and red poinsettia, or Christmas flower. Orchids are in a class of their own, and countless varieties grow in the regions around Veracruz. Bushes of pink oleander, mauve blossoms of the jacaranda tree, and the magnificent blooms of the tulipan, or African tulip tree, are also part of the Mexican scene. But most striking are the vivid scarlet blossoms of the tabuchín tree, also known as the Flame Tree, whose bursts of color brighten up even the most unexpected places.

Cacti in all their prickly forms – tall or squat, simple or multi-branched, rounded or gauntly angled – are a familiar sight. Dramatic cacti-strewn landscapes can be seen in the north-western Sonoran Desert and in Baja California, which alone boasts 120 species. Cardons, the tallest, belong to the saguaro family from Arizona. Some cacti are put to practical use: the maguey for making *tequila* and *mezcal,* the *gobernadoras* for producing rubber, the *biznaga* (barrel cactus) for water in an emergency, and the *pitahaya dulce* (organ pipes) for nectar once favored by local Indians.

Vast tracts of forest characterize many parts of the country (although the clearing of the rain forest for cultivation in regions like Chiapas is the subject of great concern). Beautiful pine woods grow all over the country, especially in the central highlands and in north-western Mexico. A great variety of trees, including the *ceiba* (kapok), and other vegetation grow in and around the humid jungles, and palm trees line the beaches. In the tropical coastal regions, there are bulrushes and mangroves, and plantations of sugar cane, coffee, cocoa beans, and tropical fruits such as bananas, mangoes, papayas, limes, pineapples, and oranges.

Wildlife

It is claimed that a thousand or so different species of birds have been recorded at some time or other in Mexico. Birds of prey include species of hawks, vultures, kestrels, and falcons.

Prickly pear: both leaves and fruit are edible

Among the many water birds you might see by the coast, on lagoons or by rivers, are graceful herons, gulls, ospreys, and terns. In the Yucatán, pink flamingos live in protected colonies. In a more domestic setting, hotel gardens can be a good place for observing varieties of woodpecker and delightful, hovering hummingbirds.

The southeastern jungles shelter members of the parrot family, including toucans and the brilliantly colored *guacamayas* (macaws). A jewel among birds is the shy quetzal, which played an important role in Mayan mythology.

Crocodiles and tarantulas are natives you will want to admire from a safe distance

A saucy look from a yellow-necked parrot

Butterflies abound, and can be seen in their thousands at the butterfly sanctuaries in Michoacán (see page 141).

The tropical forests of Chiapas are home to a host of animals, including the jaguar, ocelot, lynx, tapir, howler and spider monkeys, deer, boar, coati, and armadillos. Some are endangered species and can be seen in the magnificent free-roaming zoo in Tuxtla Gutiérrez (see page 159), created to protect the animals of the region. One remaining branch of the bear family, the small black bear, can still be seen in several states of northern Mexico, as can wolves, elks, and coyotes.

Baja California is the habitat of the elegant but rarely sighted mountain lion, or puma, and bighorn sheep live in remote desert areas.

By the shores of that rugged peninsula, you can also see colonies of California sea lions and the large gray whales that come down every winter to breed in the lagoons of the Pacific. Aquatic animals are plentiful elsewhere as well. The crocodile (*caimán*) inhabits tropical rivers, and turtles are much in evidence in the Caribbean.

There are many species of snakes, of which a number are dangerous. These include the small coral snake (*coralillo*), various species of rattlesnake (*cascabel*), and the boa constrictor.

Huge areas of undeveloped land are being designated Biosphere Reserves by the Mexican Government, providing ideal conditions for observing wildlife in its natural habitat (see pages 140–1).

History

50,000 BC
The first people are believed to arrive in America from Asia, across the Bering Strait.

10,000 BC
Tepexpan Man. The earliest human remains found in Mexico.

1200–200 BC
Pre-classic period. Olmec culture develops around the Gulf of Mexico region, particularly at San Lorenzo, La Venta, and Tres Zapotes.

AD 200–900
Classic period. Flowering of Meso-american art, ceramics, writing and the invention of the calendar. Outstanding are those of Teotihuacán and the Maya, who develop a highly advanced culture. Other cultures flourish at Monte Albán and Mitla (Oaxaca) and El Tajín (Gulf Coast).

900–1521
Post-classic period. Decline of Mayan cities and rise of the Toltecs in Tula, who migrate to the Yucatán in the 12th century and develop a Toltec–Maya culture. Mixtecs at Mitla and Monte Albán.

1325–45
The Aztecs found the capital city of Tenochtitlán. A dominant Mexica empire grows, wielding influence and power over a wide region.

1511
Shipwrecked Spaniard Gerónimo de Aguilar is captured by Yucatán Mayas; he later becomes intrepreter for Cortés.

1519
Hernán Cortés sets sail from Cuba and lands near Veracruz. He marches with about 500 men to the Aztec capital of Tenochtitlán. Emperor Moctezuma is imprisoned and killed. Bitter fighting ensues for two years.

1521
The fall of Tenochtitlán and the end of the Aztec civilization. Completion of the Conquest of "New Spain" and start of the colonial period. A new capital is built and called México.

1524
Twelve Franciscan friars arrive to set up missions.

1535
First Spanish Viceroy arrives.

1692
Insurrection in Mexico City: the Viceroy's Palace and City Hall are set ablaze by mobs.

1767
The Jesuits are expelled from Spain and its empire by order of Carlos III.

1804
All Church property is expropriated by the Crown.

1810
Father Hidalgo's famous rallying cry, *El Grito de Dolores*, signals the outbreak of the War of Independence against Spain.

1821
Agustín de Iturbide enters Mexico City with the Three Guarantee Army (one religion, solidarity among all social groups, and an independent constitutional monarchy). The Treaty of Córdoba is signed, confirming Mexico's independence after 11 years of bitter fighting.

1822
The First Empire: General Iturbide declares himself Emperor of Mexico.

1824
The monarchy is dissolved and a constitution is adopted.

1836
Texas, New Mexico, Arizona, and California declare independence from Mexico.

1846–8
Following conflict over Texas, war breaks out between the United States and Mexico. Mexico City falls to the Americans. Santa Ana resigns as President. Under the Treaty of Guadalupe, Mexico recognizes the independence of Texas, New Mexico, Arizona, and California in exchange for a sum of money.

1858
Benito Juárez becomes President. Reform Laws instituted.

1862
Mexico's suspension of repayments on its external debt leads to joint intervention by Britain, France, and Spain. France continues with military action; the French army is defeated in Puebla in the Battle of the 5th of May.

1863–4
The French take Mexico City and offer the Imperial Crown of Mexico to the Habsburg Archduke Maximilian.

1864–7
The Second Empire: Maximilian reigns briefly as Emperor of Mexico. Wars in Europe result in French troops withdrawing from Mexico. Maximilian is captured by Juárez's troops in Querétaro and executed on the Hill of Bells. The Republic is reinstated and Juárez is elected President.

1876
Porfirio Díaz is elected President. His long term of office is marked by foreign investment, development, and growth, but also increasing discontent over land ownership and other injustices.

1910
The outbreak of the Mexican Revolution, led by Francisco Madero.

Díaz flees the country and Madero assumes the Presidency but is assassinated in 1913. Bitter fighting, assassinations, and changes of presidents continue for 10 years.

1917
The New Constitution comes into effect, and is still in force today.

1919
Emiliano Zapata, fighter for agrarian reforms, is assassinated.

1920
The Revolution officially ends.

1938
President Lázaro Cárdenas expropriates British and American oil companies and nationalizes oil.

1946–52
The presidency of Miguel Alemán Valdés is a period of economic growth and tourism development.

1976–82
Under the administration of President José López Portillo, the *peso* is devalued and banks are nationalized. The country plunges into economic and political crisis.

1985
A major earthquake takes a high death toll in Mexico City.

1986
Carlos Salinas de Gortari becomes President.

1994
The North American Free Trade Agreement (NAFTA) takes effect.
A peasant uprising breaks out in Chiapas.
Assassination of Luis Donaldo Colosio, the PRI's presidential candidate.
Ernesto Zedillo Ponce de Leon assumes the presidency.
Peso devaluation causes economic crisis.

1997
PRD Cuauhtémoc Cárdenas is elected mayor of Mexico City.

Spanish Rule

*I*n 1519, the Aztec Empire controlled the entire Valley of Mexico, and its influence extended even farther. Tenochtitlán, the Aztec capital, was a city of some 300,000 inhabitants. So how could Hernán Cortés, with just 500 men and 16 horses, bring about the downfall of such an established power? A number of factors made this astonishing feat possible. Cortés, with perhaps unwitting perception, burnt his ships after landing, thus ensuring that the Spaniards would conquer or die. This suited most of his men, many of whom were determined to make their fortunes in the New World.

The Spaniards had no idea of the immense number of Indians they were challenging, not only Aztecs but uncounted hordes of other tribesmen. The Aztecs maintained their dominance through constant warfare with these other tribes, who resented their subjugation and demands for heavy tributes. As they progressed towards the capital, the Spaniards fostered alliances with some of the tribes, notably the Tlaxcalano, who swelled their ranks and made an important contribution to the ultimate success of the venture. They were also greatly aided by two interpreters: Gerónimo de Aguilar, a shipwrecked Spaniard captured by the Maya eight years earlier, and his mistress La Malinche, one of 20 maidens offered to Cortés in Tabasco, who was fluent in Maya and Náhuatl.

Cortés was helped, too, by the superstitious awe with which the Indians regarded both the Europeans and their horses. This gave the Spaniards time to establish a relatively secure toe-hold on the Aztec capital and imprison the Emperor Moctezuma, who anxiously interpreted various prophesies and portents in the light of this invasion.

Battles and skirmishes continued, however, and during one of these Moctezuma was killed. His death, on top of the unendurable edict prohibiting human sacrifice, roused the Aztecs to such an extent that Cortés retreated from Tenochtitlán. About a year later, after numerous reinforcements and more battles with various tribes, Cortés returned to the capital in 1521, to defeat the Aztecs once and for all. He razed the temples and used the stones to build churches and homes in a new city he

HERNÁN CORTÉS

1485 – Cortés is born in Medellín, Spain.

1504 – Cortés sails to Hispaniola (now the Dominican Republic).

1511 – Cortés forms part of an expedition that conquers Cuba.

1519 – Cortés sets sail for present-day Mexico with 11 ships, about 500 soldiers, some Cubans, and 16 horses. Puts ashore at San Juan de Ulúa, near Veracruz. Heads for the Aztec capital of Tenochtitlán, enters, and is received by Emperor Moctezuma.

1519–21 – two years of bitter fighting ensues. On August 13, after a final battle, Tenochtitlán falls, and Cortés takes his place in history as the conqueror of Mexico.

called México. The task of settling the whole country met with bitter resistance in some areas, but was completed by about 1600.

The Conquistadores' official purpose in conquering the land they called New Spain was to convert the natives to Christianity, but individually they aimed for a new life of wealth. Discovering silver, gold, and other minerals, the Spaniards opened lucrative mines. They also developed agriculture along European lines, and formed large feudal estates. In both cases, local Indians provided cheap labor.

The religious conquest by the missionaries, however, was as significant as the Spaniards' military triumph. Franciscans, Jesuits, Dominicans, and Augustinians dealt with the natives directly, learned their languages, earned their trust, converted the majority, and so paved the way for the fusion of the two cultures.

Thus began 300 years of relentless colonization and rule by Spain. Virtually every major city in present-day Mexico was surveyed and planned during the 16th century, following a pattern that continues to this day. Cities in New Spain centered on a plaza around which were located the church, government buildings, and business and professional premises; eventually these plazas acquired trees, fountains, and almost always a bandstand, to become the town's focus of social activities.

Over time, the society was divided into four ethnic categories: the *peninsulares* or *gachupines* (Spaniards born in Spain); *criollos* (of Spanish blood, but born in Mexico); *mestizos* (mixed Spanish and Indian, by far the largest ethnic group today); and the *indígenas* (Indians).

This relief carving shows Cortés and his men, with their Indian allies entering Mexico City

By the early 19th century resentment had increased against the *gachupines*, the elite class. In 1808, responding to hundreds of real and perceived indignities, a group formed to talk about breaking with Spain. A series of events led to the rallying cry for independence, Father Miguel Hidalgo's famous *grito*, on September 16, 1810: "My children, … Will you be free? Will you make the effort to recover from the hated Spaniards the lands stolen from you 300 years ago?…" After 10 years of fighting, the Mexicans won their independence.

Culture

*M*exico has three major eras: pre-Columbian (circa 1500 BC–AD 1521), colonial (1521–1821), and contemporary (from 1821 onwards). Traveling around the country is inevitably a journey into the complexities of its history.

Pre-Columbian cultures

Some 3,000 years ago, at the southern edge of the Gulf of Mexico, the Olmecs emerged as the first great civilization in Mesoamerica. This mother culture flourished until around 400 BC, and its achievements influenced other civilizations (notably those of Monte Albán, the Maya, and the Aztecs). Their class system, with power and knowledge concentrated in a single group, was the prototype for later societies.

Mosaic on the University Library, Mexico City

Over the centuries, other civilizations rose and fell. The artistic influence of the Teotihuacán culture covered a wide area. The Zapotecs and Mixtecs, who inhabited the valley of Oaxaca, were skilled potters and craftsmen who covered their buildings with carvings and mosaics. The Maya achieved great sophistication in astronomy, mathematics, and architecture. The last and greatest of these civilizations was that of the Aztecs, or Mexicas. By the time the Spaniards arrived, they were well advanced in sculpture, engineering, and picture-writing. Surviving from the Maya and Náhuatl cultures are many well-preserved documents containing myths, legends, proverbs, and riddles.

Warfare was a way of life in Mesoamerica, and torture and human sacrifice were used not only in religious rituals, but also in sporting events and building dedications.

Colonial art

The Conquest of Mexico saw the birth of a new cultural era. Art forms found expression in the context of the Christian religion, styles of architecture progressed from baroque to Churrigueresque (an ornate extension of baroque) and, in a minor way, neo-classical. An early type of decoration was called plateresque (from the Spanish word for silversmith, *platero*), because of the finely carved ornamental motifs.

Some churches, notably around Puebla, are the work of Indians, whose skills were recognized and encouraged by the Spaniards.

The Mural Movement

After Independence in 1821, the tradition of adorning religious buildings with carvings and murals was lost for nearly a century. The 1910–20 Revolution saw its revival. Painters were commissioned to create murals on public buildings to teach Mexican history. The great figures of this school were Diego Rivera, José Clemento Orozco, and David Siqueiros. Rufino Tamayo, their contemporary, worked independently. Influences from the past are also clearly visible in the works of more contemporary muralists, such as Juan O'Gorman, who used hundreds of mosaics for his famous building in the nation's capital, the Library at University City.

Old traditions

Native music and traditions are still maintained in some areas, often combined with Spanish or other influences. The *fiestas* held year round throughout Mexico are the best example. Many of the colorful handicrafts you can see today are produced by local artisans using techniques that have been handed down for centuries. Each region in

QUETZALCÓATL

The cult of this god (the plumed, or feathered, serpent) developed in Teotihuacán and continued among the Toltecs, Maya, and Aztecs. Mixcóatl, the first leader of the Toltec people, had a son who took the name of Quetzalcóatl, became leader of the Toltecs, and founded their new capital (present-day Tula) around AD 999.

According to one story, he threw himself on to a funeral pyre on the beach and ascended to the skies to become the morning star and ruler of time. Another story says he set out to sea on a raft of snakes and vanished, while yet another relates that he reached the Yucatán, where the cult of Quetzalcóatl (or Kukulcán) was introduced by the Maya culture. When Quetzalcóatl set sail, he vowed to return from the east and claim his land. The year prophesied for this coincided with the arrival of Cortés and his band in 1519.

Mexico has its own distinctive costumes. Traditional attire is still worn daily by some indigenous peoples, such as the Tarahumaras in the northwest, the Yucatecan women, and various groups in Chiapas. In other places, these are brought out only for *fiestas* and special occasions. One of the most attractive garments is the *china poblana* from Puebla, considered the national costume of Mexico.

Ancient stone carving,
Museum of Anthropology,
Mexico City

Politics

Mexico's political system has basically followed the same line since the late 1920s. Under the Constitution of 1917, the President is elected for a single six-year term and appoints his Cabinet ministers. The legislative body of government is the Congress of the Union, which consists of the Chamber of Deputies and the Senate.

The political party in power for nearly 70 years, the Partido Revolucionario Institucional, or PRI (originally the PNR), reigned supreme until the elections of 1988, when other parties began to gain strength.

Carlos Salinas de Gortari, who was elected President by a narrow margin, introduced radical economic and political measures to address some of Mexico's structural problems. He set up an ambitious privatization program and strongly promoted NAFTA (the North American Free Trade Agreement) between Mexico, the U.S. and Canada. Mexico seemed poised for change. But the grave problems of worsening inequalities still remained. Then its stability was severely shaken by a series of events.

As NAFTA took effect on January 1, 1994, an uprising of guerrillas broke out in Chiapas. Calling themselves the Zapatista National Liberation Army (EZLN), they made demands for economic change, land and autonomy. Violent clashes ensued with the Federal Army. The assassinations of Luis Donaldo Colosio, the PRI's popular presidential candidate, and another senior PRI official deeply shocked the nation. At the end of the year, the *peso* fell.

When Ernesto Zedillo assumed the presidency in December, 1994, he faced many problems. The devaluation of the *peso* caused an economic and confidence crisis, resulting in the negotiation of a financial aid package with the U.S. and major multilateral international agencies. Ongoing peace talks between the Zapatistas and the government have not yet succeeded in resolving the situation in Chiapas.

The mid-term elections of July, 1997 marked a crucial turning point in the history of the PRI. With the election of the PRI candidate, Cuauhtémoc Cárdenas, the PRI found itself facing an opposition mayor in Mexico City, and an opposition-dominated lower house of Congress. The right-wing PAN now governs several states and controls the majority of Mexico's larger cities.

While Mexico's political scene is undergoing change, its direction is clearly towards a more open system.

Lowering the Mexican flag as the sun goes down

FIRST STEPS

*"It is certainly among the
most varied and beautiful
in the world, as its people
are among the most
mysterious and, in their
odd prickly way, the most
likeable and attractive."*

JOHN LINCOLN
One Man's Mexico, 1967

First Steps

*M*exico is like a kaleidoscope, with many sides to its nature. No two people will see it alike. There are plenty of misconceptions about the country, and sometimes a lack of knowledge. If you go with an open mind and a positive attitude, you will be well rewarded. A sense of adventure helps too! Don't expect anything to be like it is back home – it won't be. Better to expect the unexpected. As the song claims, with good reason: "*Como México no hay dos*," "There's no other place like Mexico!"

Culture shock

Arrival at Mexico City airport is, in itself, quite an experience. A great barrage of faces hits you as you emerge. Mexican families and their children come here *en masse* to await their relatives and friends, or just to enjoy the atmosphere. Porters try to grab your bags, and there is a general air of frenzied activity.

Mexico City takes some adjusting to. Its high altitude (over 6,500 feet above sea level) and serious air pollution must be taken into account (many visitors experience sore or dry throats). Take things at a slower pace than usual, and try not to cram too much into the first couple of days or so. The city is always bustling with people. The continuous movement and noise may well seem rather overwhelming until you start to get into the spirit of things.

Etiquette and social customs

Mexicans are known for their carefree attitude and capacity to enjoy life, along with a great sense of humor. They are generally warm and friendly and more than willing to be helpful. But here you must be prepared for the fact that, while a question will always get a reply of some sort, it may not be the right one at all, as the emphasis is often on pleasing you rather than accuracy!

People here much appreciate the little

Chores in progress at a Saturday market

courtesies in life, so that *gracias* (thank you) and *de nada* (you're welcome) feature regularly in the course of conversation. They also believe in proper greetings with handshakes, or an *abrazo* (a hug) between friends, both on arrival and when taking their leave.

Like many, the Mexicans' pride in their country can become over-nationalistic at times. And while they

THOMAS COOK'S
Mexico

Cook's began to advertize Mexico as a tourist destination in 1885, following the opening of the railway between the United States and Mexico City, and the resumption of diplomatic relations between Mexico and Britain. The first Cook's agency in Mexico City opened the same year at Calle San Francisco, providing a foreign exchange service and hotel accommodation advice. Mexico soon became a popular winter resort, and a Cook's brochure for 1891–2 promised visitors "every attraction possessed by the famous resorts of the Old World together with many charming features peculiar to itself."

Young and old waiting patiently for *mañana*

themselves can be critical of its shortcomings, they do not always take kindly to criticism from others.

The indigenous people of Mexico have a very different temperament. Although not normally unfriendly, they tend to be shy and humble, preferring to keep to themselves. They also have great dignity and should always be treated with courtesy and consideration.

Family life
Life in Mexico revolves around the family, which takes priority above everything else. There are strong feelings of love and loyalty within families, and they go to extraordinary lengths to help one another. Children are very much cared for and they, in turn,

show great respect for their parents.

Although Mexicans generally entertain out, they are a naturally hospitable people. The expression "*Usted tiene su casa*" (This is your home) is a commonly used courtesy. It can lead to a genuine invitation to come home and meet the family – and when it does, you know you have really been taken into their hearts.

Linguistic nuances

You can get by in good restaurants, hotels, and some shops in Mexico City and in tourist centers without any knowledge of Spanish. English is not normally spoken in more modest restaurants. Some effort on your part is always appreciated, however, even if it only amounts to such basics as *buenos días* (good morning), *buenas noches* (goodnight) and, most important, *gracias* (thank you).

Naturally, you stand to gain if you speak some Spanish. Apart from helping in sorting out problems, you can learn all sorts of interesting local information from taxi drivers, barmen, or other local people. Traveling independently off the beaten track becomes difficult if you don't speak the language. In addition to Spanish, a number of different languages and dialects are still spoken by the various Indian groups in their regions. These are mostly away from the usual tourist areas, with the exception of Mérida, and in the Yucatán generally. If you listen carefully, you will hear the local people conversing very softly in the Mayan language.

Machismo

No account of Mexico would be complete without reference to the famous *machismo*, with which it is often associated. The Mexican *macho* tends to be portrayed as a dashing *charro* (rodeo rider) astride his horse, or swaggering into a bar with a stetson and a low-slung belt. *Machismo* is a sort of demonstration of maleness, and of outdoing other men. It manifests itself in many ways. Young men show daring by driving fast and recklessly, or by their courageous diving feats off the cliffs in Acapulco.

Most towns and villages have men-

The benches on any *zócalo* (main square) are never empty for long in fine weather

only *cantinas* and pool rooms, where women may not enter. This is not out of disrespect for women – rather to the contrary. Being a little rough, these places are felt to be inappropriate for women. Mexicans respect their women and feel protective towards them. Chivalry is still very much alive in Mexico. A man will open a door for a woman, walk on the side nearest the street and very rarely permit her to pay for a meal or a drink. When his own woman is concerned, however, protectiveness can turn into possessiveness. Should she be subject to any provocative attention from another male, the *machismo* can really show.

Women

Women are gradually becoming more emancipated in Mexico, and career-minded. However, many patriarchal traditions remain strong in contemporary Mexican culture. A woman on her own in a bar, restaurant, or public place is likely to attract attention. She would be well advised to avoid provocative clothing or behavior, and to deal with any unwelcome advances by a shake of the head, or a firm "NO"!

The *mañana* syndrome

The *mañana* mentality of leaving things until the following day, or some unspecified time, is a broadly Latin one, but it has certainly found a home in Mexico. Not surprisingly, Mexicans are fond of the saying: "Never do today what you can put off until tomorrow, and never do tomorrow what you can put off forever." It must be said, however, that the Mexican people have imagination and a feeling for improvisation. When all else seems hopeless, they have a way of getting everything done – just in time.

Wares for sale in Taxco's *zócalo*

Touts

As in many tourist countries, you may well be approached quite frequently by people who want to sell you something you don't want. In Mexico City, the travel touts work tourist areas around hotels. You will come across them in the Zona Rosa offering to guide you to the pyramids, markets, around the city, and so on. It is wise to ignore them, as they are unlikely to be registered guides, could be expensive, and may not offer what they claim. It's best to book a tour through your hotel or a reputable travel agency. Unless you want to overpay, avoid taxi touts, very visible in Mexico City, at the airport or cruising the streets in large flashy cars. Between the metered Volkswagen taxis and the *sitios* outside hotels, there is usually more than sufficient transportation available.

WHERE TO GO

If traveling independently to Mexico for the first time, you will have the task of deciding which destinations to include and, more difficult, which to leave out. Mexico offers such a diversity of attractions that it is not easy to decide. Whatever your interests, try not to cram too much in. Distances are greater than you think. The strain of travel and the climatic and altitude changes can take their toll. Besides, there is always something unexpected to see around the next corner. Allow a little extra time in each place, just in case.

Two or three weeks at least is suggested for touring around, with a few days in Mexico City to start off. There are many possibilities, depending on whether your interests lie in ancient ruins, colonial towns, mountain scenery, jungles and nature, swinging beach resorts, or more rustic hideaways. Deserts and canyons might appeal. Mexico has something for everyone.

Ancient cultures

The majority of Mexico's major archaeological sites are in the southeast. A classic tour, best done by air, includes Oaxaca, for the nearby Zapotec and Mixtec ruins of Monte Albán and Mitla; Villahermosa as a base from which to visit the spectacular jungle ruins of Palenque; and Mérida, from which you can visit the famous Mayan cities of Uxmal and Chichén Itzá. In addition, there are numerous smaller sites dotted about the region, some of which are not easily accessible.

Land only a cactus could love!

Colonial cities of Central Mexico
A delightful overland tour takes you along the Colonial Route, which includes the towns of Querétaro, San Miguel de Allende, Guanajuato, and Morelia, which are noted for their attractive architecture and historical interest in connection with the War of Independence against the Spaniards.

The Route of the Volcanoes
A trip by road east to Veracruz via Puebla and Orizaba takes you through extraordinary changes of scenery, from the high altitude of Mexico City down to the steamy Gulf region. The route offers magnificent views of Mexico's famous snow-tipped volcanoes, Popocatépetl, Iztaccíhuatl, Orizaba, and La Malinche (see page 137). Avoid the rainy summer months, when the volcanoes can be covered with clouds.

Beaches
The shores of Mexico offer tremendous choice. Along the Pacific coastline are numerous resorts, ranging from Acapulco and Puerto Vallarta to Ixtapa and the more rustic Zihuatanejo, and resort complexes such as Las Hadas and the Bel-Air Costa Careyes. Farther south, the Huatulco developement contrasts with the small resorts of Puerto Angel and Puerto Escondido. The Caribbean boasts the popular resort of Cancún and the islands of Cozumel and Isla Mujeres, along with other developments down the coast.

Deserts and canyons of the North
Mexico's northern expanses include ranching areas, deserts and cacti, and the Copper Canyon (Barranca del Cobre), homeland of the proudly traditional Tarahumara Indians. This is one of the

Artistry of another age adorns the entrance to this church in Atlixco, Morelos

most scenic and interesting areas in the country, though somewhat off the beaten track for some people. A trip on the Copper Canyon railway is most rewarding (see pages 138–9).

Baja California
If you are looking for something different, this is it. This long thin peninsula features vineyards and olive groves, deserts and mountains, cacti, wild rocks and seas, and clear blue skies. It is little populated and offers excellent swimming and big game sportfishing, water sports and a great outdoor life, plus a reliably pleasant climate.

What to wear

As a general rule, take casual and comfortable clothes. Beyond that, you must take into account climate and the nature of the area. Mexico City requires more formal clothes. Men should have a tie and jacket for upper-grade restaurants. Dressy pants for women are quite acceptable. Between December and February women may need a coat for the evening. Otherwise, a light jacket should be sufficient. Cotton is more comfortable than synthetic materials.

For touring around, make sure you have comfortable shoes for exploring cobblestone streets and ruins. Take a sweater, shawl, or light jacket for cold evenings at higher altitudes. Women do not have to cover their heads when entering a church. As for beach resorts, think cool and casual, with appropriate cover-ups as occasion demands, for example in hotel restaurants. Topless sunbathing and nude swimming are not acceptable in Mexico, nor is going barefoot on the street.

If travelling in the rainy summer season, take an anorak or light raincoat and an umbrella.

When to go

November to May is the best time to visit Mexico. You can expect a good climate, warm waters for swimming, and greener landscapes after the summer rains. The peak tourist season is about mid-December to mid-April, when hotel rates can be considerably higher in the popular coastal resorts. The summer months are hot, humid, and rainy, while September's weather can be unpredictable, with storms and the occasional hurricane, particularly in the Gulf and Caribbean and the southern half of Baja California.

Hats and canopies help keep off the heat

"*And there under an intense light sky lies a shining plain succulent with sugar-cane and corn among the cacti, a bright rich tropical country miraculously laved: green, green, green, the Valley of Mexico.*"

SYBILLE BEDFORD
A Visit to Don Octavio, 1953

Mexico City

*M*exico City (Ciudad de México), the nation's capital, has grown into a sprawling metropolis with an estimated population of 22 million (out of the country's total of 93 million). It claims to be the world's most populous city and, at 7,350 feet above sea level, is also one of the highest. You will get an idea of its size when you fly over it and see this huge conurbation, ringed by mountains, spreading across the Valley of Mexico. To arrive by night is an impressive experience, as the whole valley becomes a carpet of glittering lights.

The city was built in 1521 by the Spaniards on the ruins of the Aztec capital of Tenochtitlán. Today, it is a blend of modern skyscrapers, wide boulevards, and the old historic center with narrow streets, churches, and colonial buildings. Referred to by the Mexicans simply as México, or the Distrito Federal (DF), it is the hub of the country. The altitude can cause shortness of breath and a feeling of tiredness, but should not overly affect anyone enjoying normal good health. Smog is an unfortunate continuing problem here, and at times a thick grey pall descends over the place. There are many beautiful days, however, when you can enjoy the city under clear, blue skies.

The feel of the city

Exploring Mexico City requires both stamina and patience. Wide boulevards, large intersections, heavy traffic, and high, uneven pavements can be challenging. But it is always interesting, and full of surprises. The streets are bursting with color, noise, and activity. The most suitable areas for strolling about are the historic center around the Zócalo, the Zona Rosa, along the Paseo de la Reforma, and Chapultepec Park. In some districts, the streets names follow particular themes, such as famous cities (in the Zona Rosa), rivers, or great

writers, poets, and philosophers; this can help in locating the neighborhood.

Mexico City skyline from Chapultepec Castle

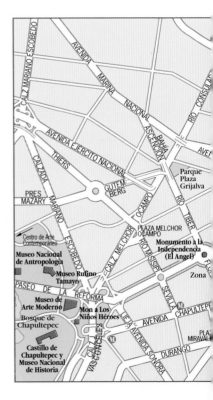

MEXICO CITY

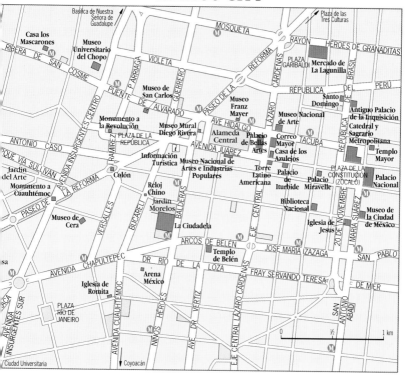

Basílica de Nuestra Señora de Guadalupe

Plaza de las Tres Culturas

MOSQUETA

RAYÓN

HÉROES DE GRANADITAS

Casa los Mascarones

Museo Universitario del Chopo

RIBERA DE SAN COSME

VIOLETA

REFORMA

CÁRDENAS

PLAZA GARIBALDI

Mercado de La Lagunilla

BRASIL

P. ARRIAGA

GUERRERO

PASEO DE LA

REPÚBLICA

PERÚ

PUENTE DE

ALVARADO

Museo de San Carlos

Museo Franz Mayer

Santo Domingo

DEL

Antiguo Palacio de la Inquisición

REPÚBLICA

ANTONIO CASO

AVENIDA INSURGENTES CENTRO

Monumento a la Revolución

Museo Mural Diego Rivera

AVE HIDALGO

LÁZARO

Museo Nacional de Arte

Catedral y Sagrario Metropolitana

PLAZA DE LA REPÚBLICA

Alameda Central

Palacio de Bellas Artes

Correo Mayor

TACUBA

Templo Mayor

RAMÍREZ

AVENIDA JUÁREZ

Casa de los Azulejos

PARQUE VÍA SULLIVAN

Jardín del Arte

Información Turística

Museo Nacional de Artes e Industrias Populares

Torre Latino Americana

Palacio de Iturbide

Palacio Miravelle

PLAZA DE LA CONSTITUCIÓN (ZÓCALO)

Palacio Nacional

Colón

Monumento a Cuauhtémoc

LA REFORMA

Reloj Chino

Jardín Morelos

Biblioteca Nacional

Iglesia de Jesús

20 DE NOVIEMBRE

MARÍA JUÁREZ

Museo de la Ciudad de México

PASEO DE

VERSALLES

BUCARELI

BALDERAS

La Ciudadela

EJE CENTRAL

ARCOS DE BELÉN

JOSÉ MARÍA IZAZAGA

SAN PABLO

Museo de Cera

AVENIDA CHAPULTEPEC

DR RÍO DE LA LOZA

Templo de Belén

FRAY SERVANDO TERESA

DE MIER

Iglesia de Romita

AVENIDA CUAUHTÉMOC

NIÑOS HÉROES

Arena México

AVE. DR VERTIZ

EJE CENTRAL LÁZARO CÁRDENAS

SAN ANTONIO ABAD

AVENIDA INSURGENTES SUR

PLAZA RÍO DE JANEIRO

0   ½   1 km

Ciudad Universitaria

Coyoacán

Chapultepec Castle, now a museum, proudly surveys its parkland setting

ALAMEDA CENTRAL

This is Mexico City's central park, dating back to the end of the 16th century. Graceful bronze Italian statues adorn the attractive park, which has paths, fountains, and many varieties of trees. In front stands an impressive marble monument to President Benito Juárez. On Sundays, the place teems with Mexican families taking a stroll.

Between Avenida Juárez and Avenida Hidalgo. Open: daily. Free. Metro: Bellas Artes or Hidalgo.

BASÍLICA DE NUESTRA SEÑORA DE GUADALUPE

The Basílica of Our Lady of Guadalupe is regarded as the holiest place in Mexico (see page 47). According to legend, it was here, in December 1531, that an Indian boy, Juan Diego, saw a vision of the Virgin Mary, who asked that a church be built in her honor. When advised of this, the local bishop asked for proof. The Virgin appeared again, asking the boy to gather some roses from near by. This he did, and when he opened his cloak to show them to the bishop, the beautiful image of the dark-skinned Virgin was imprinted on it. A church was built on this site and consecrated as a shrine, with the Virgin of Guadalupe declared the Patron Saint of Mexico.

The imposing old basilica, which was sinking into the subsoil, has been replaced by a contemporary-style building designed by Pedro Ramírez Vázquez. A moving stairway takes you slowly past the Virgin's image on the Indian's cloak. The shrine is the object of year-round pilgrimages from all over Mexico and beyond.

10km north of downtown Mexico City. Open: daily 6am–9pm. Free. Metro: Basílica.

BOSQUE DE CHAPULTEPEC

Chapultepec Park is an area of over 2,000 acres of parklands, with woods, fields, and lakes. Used by the Aztecs, it is one of the oldest natural parks in North America. It features magnificent *ahuehuetes* (giant cypress trees), some of which are centuries old. Mexicans bring their children here on a Sunday to enjoy the amusement park, the zoo, and boating on the lake. Located in the park are the Museum of Anthropology (see pages 32–3), Chapultepec Castle, and other museums (see pages 34–5).

West of Mexico City. Open: daily. Metro: Chapultepec.

CASTILLO DE CHAPULTEPEC

Chapultepec Castle stands high up on a hill, overlooking the Park and Mexico City, with a magnificent view of the Paseo de la Reforma. First built as a castle in the 18th century, it later became a military academy and in 1847 was the scene of a battle with U.S. troops, during which six young cadets died defending the school. An impressive monument in front of the castle, Los Niños Héroes

(The Young Heroes), commemorates the event.

The Habsburg Emperor Maximilian and his wife, Carlotta, resided here during his short reign (1864–7). It now functions as the National Museum of History, with interesting relics of the life and times of Maximilian and varied displays of art and ordinary objects depicting Mexican life, from the Conquest to 1917.
Section 1 of Chapultepec Park. Tel: 286–07–00/99–20. Open: Tuesday to Sunday 9am–5pm. Admission charge.

CATEDRAL METROPOLITANA
The Metropolitan Cathedral – the largest in Latin America – stands on the Zócalo, the capital's main square. It is an imposing edifice, constructed on the site of an earlier church, built in 1525, by the Spaniards following the Conquest, and later demolished in favor of the present cathedral. It took some 250 years to complete, and hence presents various styles of architecture. Adjoining it is the Sagrario (Sacrarium), built in the mid-1700s in rich baroque style.

North side of the Zócalo. Open: daily 8am–6pm. Free.

CIUDAD UNIVERSITARIA
University City, located south of the center in the Pedregal District, is the campus of the Universidad Nacional Autónoma de México (National Autonomous University of Mexico – UNAM), where over 300,000 students are registered. The original university was founded in 1553, to be replaced in time by the current institution. The present campus, built in the 1950s, is noted for its striking modern architecture and bold murals. Buildings outstanding for their design and murals are, among others, the mosaic-covered Central Library, masterpiece of Juan O'Gorman, the School of Medicine, the Rector's Office, and the Auditorium of the Science Faculty..
Off Insurgentes Sur, 11km south of Paseo de la Reforma. Metro: Universidad.

The Catedral, with statues of Faith, Hope, and Charity on top of the clock tower

Museo Nacional de Antropología

*T*he National Museum of Anthropology is a must for any visitor to Mexico City. Its unique collection of pre-Columbian art treasures, magnificently presented, places it among the world's finest museums of this kind. Opened in 1964, it was designed by renowned Mexican architect Pedro Ramírez Vázquez, centering around a courtyard which features a single pillar supporting a huge umbrella-like concrete roof. A dramatic waterfall drops in a translucent sheet, while a huge monolithic sculpture, believed to portray Tláloc, the god of rain, stands at the entrance surrounded by water.

The museum has three floors. On the lower ground level is the Orientation Room, where you can see models and films on Mesoamerican culture. On the upper floor, the Ethnography Section has a number of halls showing the way of life of the various Indian groups living in Mexico today. The ground floor, however, forms the major part of the museum. Exhibition halls around the patio are devoted to the fascinating pre-Hispanic period, from earliest settlements to the blossoming of advanced civilizations. A walk around counter-clockwise takes you in and out of the various halls with restful pauses.

Hall 1 offers an Introduction to Anthropology, with exhibits and drawings of the evolution of humans. This leads to Halls 2 and 3, named Mesoamerica and the Origins. Halls 4 and 5 cover the Pre-Classic Period and Teotihuacán, with drawings, models, and pottery from these civilizations.

The Toltec Hall (No. 6) includes an impressive Atlantean warrior figure from Tula, stelae (carved stone slabs or pillars), and sculptures. Outside, at the rear of the hall, is part of a temple from Tula, decorated and colored.

Taking center stage at the far end of the complex is Hall 7, the México Hall. This is one of the most exciting areas, dealing with the Aztec, or México, culture. Facing you, high up on a white marble slab, is the famous Sun Stone (or Aztec Calendar, as it is often called), depicting the face of the Sun God, Tonatiuh, surrounded by hieroglyphs of days and months interspersed with solar rays. Undoubtedly a highlight of the museum, it imbues the hall with a sense of solemnity and ancient magic. Also prominently displayed are important sculptures recovered from the Templo Mayor

The feathered serpent god, Quetzalcóatl

Detailed carvings like this one are rich in clues about Mexico's pre-Hispanic societies

excavations on the Zócalo. Other impressive exhibits in the hall are the model (and painting above it) of the Aztec capital of Tenochtitlán, and the reproduction of Emperor Moctezuma's plumes.

Continuing around the block you will come to the Oaxaca Hall (No. 8), which features many small figurines, urns, and stelae from the Zapotec and Mixtec cultures. This leads to the Gulf of Mexico Hall (No. 9), where you are confronted by a giant Olmec monolithic head, its Negroid features pitted with tiny holes, found in San Lorenzo, Veracruz. The hall covers the period from 1200–600 BC and contains many

intriguing sculptures, including some curious Huastecan figures.

The Maya Hall (No. 10) is of great interest, featuring large masks found in the state of Campeche, stone carvings from Chichén Itzá, figurines from Jaina, and copies of the famous Bonampak frescos. The remaining two halls deal with the cultures of the North and the West.

Northern section of Chapultepec Park, on Paseo de la Reforma and Gandhi. Tel: 553–19–02/63–81/63–86. Open: Tuesday to Saturday 9am–7pm, Sunday 10am–6pm. Admission charge (Sundays free). Cameras without flash are permitted. Guides speaking other languages can be hired on request.

MUSEUMS

In addition to the famous Museum of Anthropology, the city has a number of museums devoted to history, art, and other subjects. Unless stated otherwise, they are open daily except for Monday.

Museo de Anahuacalli

The House of Anahuac was designed by Diego Rivera and has a collection of pre-Columbian art and sketches by the artist. *Calle del Museo 150, Coyoacán. Tel: 617–43–10. Open: 10am–6pm. Admission charge.*

Papier-mâché skeleton at Anahuacalli Museum

Centro Cultural de Arte Contemporáneo

Temporary exhibitions of international and Mexican artists. *Corner of Campos Elíseos and Calle Jorge Elliot, Chapultepec Park. Tel: 282–03–55. Open: Tuesday and Thursday to Sunday 10am–6pm (until 9pm on Wednesday). Admission charge.*

Museo de Arte Moderno

The Museum of Modern Art has works by notable 19th- and 20th-century Mexican artists, also temporary exhibitions. *Paseo de la Reforma y Gandhi. Tel: 553–62–33. Open: Tuesday to Sunday 10am–6pm. Admission charge.*

Museo de la Ciudad de México

Museum of the city's history, housed in an attractive former mansion. *Pino Suárez 30, Zócalo area. Tel: 542–04–87. Open: 10am–6pm. Admission charge.*

Museo Franz Mayer

Franz Mayer's collection of European, Asiatic, and American artifacts. *Avenida Hidalgo 45, Zócalo area. Tel: 518–22–65/66/67. Open: 10am–5pm. Admission charge.*

Museo Frida Kahlo

Works by Frida Kahlo, her husband Diego Rivera, and other Mexican artists. *Londres 247, Coyoacán. Tel: 554–59–99. Open: 10am–6pm. Admission charge.*

Museo Mural Diego Rivera

This museum was built especially to house the famous Diego Rivera mural (*Dream of a Sunday Afternoon in Alameda Central*) at the Del Prado Hotel, moved after the devastating 1985 earthquake. *Balderas and Colón, Plaza Solidarid. Tel: 512–07–54. Open: 10am–6pm. Free.*

Museo Nacional de Antropología

See pages 32–3.

Museo Nacional de Historia

See Castillo de Chapultepec, page 30.

Museo Rufino Tamayo

This museum houses the art collection of Rufino Tamayo and includes paintings by

Belying its 20th-century construction, the Palace of Fine Arts offers a grand welcome

international and Mexican artists.
Paseo de la Reforma y Gandhi. Tel: 286–35–72/58–39/65–19. Open: 10am–6pm. Admission charge.

PALACIO DE BELLAS ARTES

This opulent, white marble Palace of Fine Arts was built between 1905 and 1934. Home of the national opera and symphony orchestra, it is also famous for its twice-weekly performances of the brilliant Mexican National Ballet Folklórico. A striking feature is the glass curtain made by Tiffany's of New York, depicting the volcanoes Popocatépetl and Iztaccíhuatl.
Avenida Juárez. Tel: 510–13–88/709–31–11. Open: 10am–6pm. Admission charge.

PALACIO NACIONAL

Standing atop the old Aztec ruins, the building has seen several changes. From 1698 to Independence in 1821, it was the home of the Spanish Viceroys, since when it has housed the offices of the President of Mexico. The bell which hangs over the central porch is said to be the one rung by Father Miguel Hidalgo, the parish priest of Dolores (Guanajuato), when he rallied the populace in 1810 to take up the struggle against the Spaniards. Inside, adorning the walls over the central staircase, are magnificent Diego Rivera murals depicting the history of Mexico.
Eastern side of the Zócalo. Open: 9am–5pm.

Rivera's mural is a study in social history

The broad and leafy Reforma is a window on the world, with its never-ceasing bustle

PASEO DE LA REFORMA

This is Mexico City's most famous boulevard. Extending for 15km, from Tlatelolco in the northeast to Lomas in the west, it was built at the behest of Emperor Maximilian to link Chapultepec Castle with the National Palace on the Zócalo. Known at the time as Calzada del Emperador (The Emperor's Way), it was later named Reforma after the Reform Laws of President Benito Juárez. From the hilltop castle there is a fine view of Reforma down to the Zócalo.

The main part of the boulevard, between Avenida Juárez and Chapultepec Park, is very impressive, lined with palms and other plants, and several traffic lanes on either side of a central pedestrian area. There are several traffic monstrous roundabouts (*glorietas*) and a number of monuments to honor heroes or important historical events.

Notable sculptures are those of Cuauhtémoc, the last Aztec ruler, and the Columbus monument. Most famous, however, and a landmark of Mexico City, is the Independence Monument, known simply as El Angel, because of the gilded angel that proudly crowns its imposing column.

PLAZA DE LAS TRES CULTURAS
See pages 46–7.

PLAZA GARIBALDI
A visit to this ever-popular spot will give you a real flavor of the Mexican's natural capacity for good, rousing fun. Numerous *mariachi* bands, dressed in their smart *charro* outfits, congregate in this square every evening and play requests for payment. With different groups playing simultaneously, the enjoyable cacophony creates an incredible ambience! Cantinas, restaurants, and popular night spots around the square all

add to the lively scene.
*About 10 minutes north of the Palace of
Fine Arts, east of Calle Lázaro Cárdenas.*

TORRE LATINOAMERICANA

The impressive 43-story Latin-
American Tower, the second highest
building in Mexico City, offers
panoramic views of the city and the
Valley of Mexico. Two elevators take you
up to a splendid observation deck on the
42nd floor. On a clear day there is a
good view of Popocatépetl and
Iztaccíhuatl.
*Calle Lázaro Cárdenas. Open: daily
10am–11pm. Admission charge to
observation tower.*

ZÓCALO

This is the main square of Mexico City
and the heart of the old city. Officially
named Plaza de la Constitución
(Constitution Square), it is known
simply as the Zócalo, which means
"pedestal" and refers back to the base of
as monument planned for the square,
but never built. Most main squares in
Mexico are known as the zócalo.

This vast area once boasted gardens,
fountains, trees, and a bandstand. In the
1900s, however, it was all filled with
concrete, and nowadays is adorned only
with a large Mexican flag. The Zócalo is
nevertheless most impressive, bordered
by superb buildings and full of animated
activity day and night, with native
dancers and other forms of entertainment.
Metro: Zócalo.

ZONA ROSA

The "Pink Zone" – a name whose origin
is obscure – is a compact area that runs
south of Reforma to Avenida
Chapultepec, bounded by Insurgentes to
the east and Lieja to the west. The Zona
Rosa has lost some of its trendiness to
other areas, such as Polanco, but it still
offers a lively, attractive concentration of
art galleries, elegant shops, bars and
restaurants, vendors, and music-makers.
Pedestrian streets are lined with cafés
that invite you to sit outside and watch
the world go by.

The Zócalo, looking deceptively dreary, is the
focus of much activity and entertainment

Mexico City Environs

ARCHAEOLOGICAL SITES

A number of pre-Columbian sites can be visited on a day trip from Mexico City. Most are free on Sundays and public holidays. Unless stated otherwise, they are open daily, except Monday.

Cacaxtla-Xochitécatl

This ancient ceremonial site has excited attention since the discovery of highly colored Mayan-style murals. The ruins date from around AD 200–1300. Overlooking Cacaxtla, the small ceremonial centre of Xochitécatl features four structures from the Classic period and a stunning view of the volcanoes. *About 96km east of Mexico City, 20km southwest of Tlaxcala. Open: 10am–5pm (Cacaxtla murals 10am–1pm). Admission charge.*

Calixtlahuaca

The main feature of this site is the circular Temple of Quetzalcóatl, dedicated to the wind god Ehecatl. Parts of the structures point to several cultures, including Teotihuacán, Toltec, and Aztec. *8km north of Toluca. Open: 8am–6pm.*

Cuicuilco

One of the earliest known structures in Mexico. The area was embedded in lava after a violent volcanic eruption and uncovered only in the 1920s. *Insurgentes Sur, 3km west of Tlalpan. Open: 8am–6pm.*

Malinalco

Aztec ceremonial center of dramatic structures hewn from stone, surrounded by forests, rivers, and rock formations.

12km east of Tenancingo, on Mex 55. Open: 10am–4:30pm.

Teotenango

Large site dating back to around the 7th century AD. Thought to have been an important ceremonial center. *25km north of Tenancingo, on Mex 55. Open: 9am–5pm.*

Tula

The remains of Tollan, former capital of the Toltec people, with Atlantean warrior figures that once supported the roof of a temple. Tollan was founded in AD 968 but abandoned in 1168 after being sacked by the Chichimecs, from the northern desert. *85km north of Mexico City. Open: 9am–5pm. Admission charge.*

Xochicalco

The early history of these hilltop ruins is unknown. However, evidence links them with various cultures, including Zapotec and Maya. *36km southwest of Cuernavaca. Open: 9am–5pm. Admission charge.*

OTHER ATTRACTIONS

Desierto de los Leones

A large parkland of coniferous forests with marked trails and the ruins of a 17th-century Carmelite monastery. *20km west of Mexico City. Park open: daily (free). Monastery open: Tuesday to Sunday 10am–5pm. Admission charge.*

Lagunas de Zempoala

Seven lagoons set in a national park, high in wooded mountains; a good area for walking, boating, fishing, and camping.

62km southwest of Mexico City. Open: daily. Free.

Tepotzotlán
The façade of the convent church of San Francisco Javier rates as one of Mexico's finest examples of the Churrigueresque style. The interior is highly adorned and magnificent.
42km north of Mexico City, on Mex 57. Open: 10am–5pm.

Tepoztlán
Náhuatl, the ancient tongue of the Aztecs, is still spoken here, and certain Aztec traditions are preserved in *fiestas*. On the square stands a vast 16th-century convent, built by the Dominicans. A fairly tough climb of 30 minutes up the rocky hillside takes you to the Pyramid of Tepozteco, with spectacular views.
25km northeast of Cuernavaca. Open: daily 10am–4:30pm.

MEXICO CITY ENVIRONS

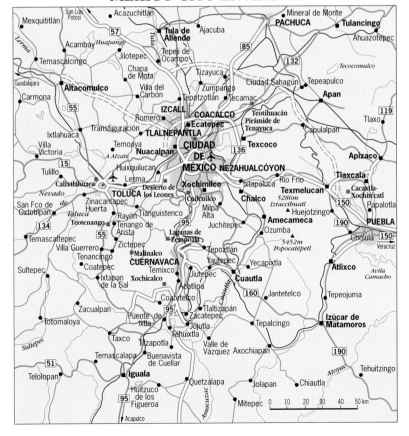

Monterrey

Guanajuato   Mérida

Mexico City   Puebla
              Oaxaca

Mexico City's Historic Center

This walk takes you down to the Zócalo, heart of old Mexico City, and is signposted as Centro Histórico (Historic Center). Sunday is a good day, when traffic is minimal. Allow 2 to 3 hours.

Start at the intersection of Paseo de la Reforma and Avenida Juárez, and walk down Avenida Juárez.

1 AVENIDA JUÁREZ

As you walk down this wide boulevard you will pass, on your left, the attractive Alameda Central (see page 30), a focal point of the city, fronted by a semi-circular monument to Reform President Benito Juárez. A little farther on is the handsome white marble Palacio de Bellas Artes (see page 35), work of the Italian architect Adamo Boari, which is renowned as a venue for the spectacular Mexican National Ballet Folklórico.

Cross over Avenida Lázaro Cárdenas and continue walking down Calle Francisco 1 Madero.

2 CALLE FRANCISCO 1 MADERO

This is an old street, and one of the most interesting in Mexico. Formerly known for its silversmiths, it still has many shops selling gold and silver jewelry. Immediately on your right, you will notice the Latin-American Tower (see page 37). Over to your left is the Casa de los Azulejos (House of Tiles). Originally built as a palace, it now houses a Sanborns restaurant and gift

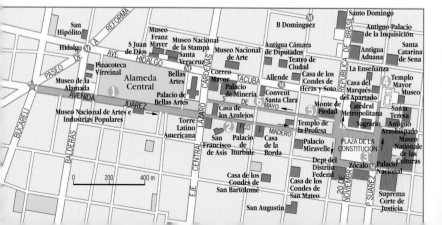

shop. On your right is the 16th-century Templo de San Francisco de Asis (Church of St. Francis of Assisi), followed by the Palacio de Iturbide. Formerly the palace of Agustín de Iturbide during his brief spell as Mexico's first emperor (1821–3), it is now a branch of Banamex (the state-owned bank), with art exhibitions held in the atrium. On the corner of the Zócalo is the Hotel Majestic, which offers a unique view of the grand square from its terrace restaurant.
Enter the Zócalo.

3 THE ZÓCALO
Officially called the Plaza de la Constitución (Constitution Square), this is usually referred to as the Zócalo – hub of Mexico City, a grandiose square full of life (see page 37). Turn right onto Calle 16 de Septiembre to take a look at the unusual interior of the Howard Johnson Gran Hotel; the bar also offers a good view. Returning to the Zócalo, you will see facing you the National Palace (see page 35), housing various Government departments. Inside, over the staircase, are the famous Diego Rivera murals depicting the history of Mexico. To the left is the Metropolitan Cathedral, with the adjoining Sagrario (see page 31).
Walk behind the cathedral to the excavations of the Templo Mayor.

4 TEMPLO MAYOR
The Aztec remains of this "Great Temple" were discovered quite by chance, in 1978, when workmen were laying cables for the metro. Excavations over the ensuing years revealed hundreds of sculptures, including some large pieces of great significance. A model displays the grandeur of

Tenochtitlán, the ancient Aztec capital.
Walk back along the other side of the cathedral, cross the road, and enter the Monte de Piedad.

Serpent's head discovered at Templo Mayor

5 MONTE DE PIEDAD
Literally meaning "Mountain of Piety," this is Mexico City's National Pawnshop – a fascinating place and well worth a visit. Dating back to 1777, it was built on the site of a former Aztec palace, as a charitable organization to help the needy. As you pass through a long arcade, you will see everything imaginable on sale, ranging from antiques and jewelry to household goods and electronic equipment.
Walk straight through. You will come out onto Calle Cinco de Mayo.

6 CALLE CINCO DE MAYO
Virtually the whole street is dedicated to books. Readers of Spanish can find all sorts of fascinating tomes here, and the booksellers are generally very willing and helpful.
You should have no problem finding a taxi here, if you wish to return to your hotel.

The Floating Gardens of Xochimilco

This tour visits some of the attractions to be found south of the capital, including the University, the Olympic Stadium, the Pedregal and San Angel districts, and a boat trip on the Floating Gardens of Xochimilco. *Allow a full day.*

Start at the intersection of Paseo de la Reforma and Insurgentes Sur, and proceed south. Take a look at the colorful, exuberant flower market on your left.

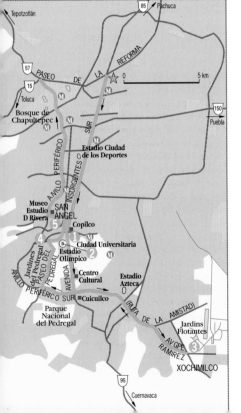

1 CIUDAD UNIVERSITARIA

Founded in the 1950s, University City (see page 31) has a large campus and some 300,000 registered students. It is worth stopping to take a look at the bold architecture and the use of murals and frescos, taken from ancient designs. Don't miss the 10-story mosaic-decorated Central Library by Juan O'Gorman, the Rector's Office, and the former Faculty of Science and the Faculty of Medicine, which are noted for their thought-provoking murals.
Cross over the road to take a look at the Olympic Stadium.

2 ESTADIO OLIMPICO

Shaped like a volcanic crater, this stadium was built for the 1968 Summer Olympics and features a mosaic mural by Diego Rivera over the main entrance, intended to be the first of a series. The stadium holds 80,000 people.
Continue south. Take the Anillo Periférico, also known as La Ruta de la Amistad (Friendship Boulevard) and take the turning to Xochimilco.

Take a ride in a shaded boat and let your guide worry about watery traffic jams

3 FLOATING GARDENS OF XOCHIMILCO

Although a typical tourist attraction, a canal tour here is colorful and fun. Sunday is the liveliest day, when Mexicans take their families out. Other boats glide past with *mariachis*, flowers and handicrafts to sell. Here you will be reminded that the city was built on a lake, as you pass through *chinampas*, artificial islands (no longer floating) on which flowers and vegetables grow. (Be sure to agree on the tour price beforehand; a party of at least three is recommended because of the cost.)

Take the Anillo Periférico northwest, cross over Insurgentes Sur, and turn right onto the Paseo del Pedregal. Continue north.

4 JARDINES DEL PEDREGAL

Formerly a volcanic wasteland, this area was transformed into a smart residential area where clever architecture has made use of the lava shapes and incorporated them into houses and gardens.

Take Avenida San Jerónimo northeast; join Avenida Revolución into San Angel district.

5 SAN ANGEL COLONIAL RESIDENTIAL AREA

This is a charming area of colonial houses and cobblestone streets. Have a look at the old Carmelite convent (No. 4), now the Museo de Carmen, with its flower-filled courtyard. Built in 1615–17, it contains an important collection of religious art, particularly baroque sculptures; the crypt contains mummified bodies. Nearby is the Plaza San Jacinto, a large square where every Saturday sees the Bazar Sábado. This is a vast craft center, with stalls set up on the square itself and in surrounding buildings. Handicrafts come from all over Mexico, and the standard is high. While here, have a meal or a drink in the San Angel Inn, a beautifully restored 18th-century *hacienda* in Altavista.

Turn west on to the Anillo Periférico and return north to Mexico City.

The Aztecs

*A*ccording to legend, the Aztecs originated from the mythical Aztlán, believed to be the tiny island of Mexcaltitán, on the northwest coast of Mexico. The Aztecs, or Mexica, as they also called themselves, wandered long before arriving in the Valley of Mexico (Anáhuac) during the course of the 12th century AD. They settled in Chapultepec (Hill of the Grasshoppers) until around 1325, when, following a prophecy of their god Huitzilopochtli, they saw an eagle on a cactus eating a snake in the middle of Lake Texcoco, and founded their capital Tenochtitlán there.

The Aztecs went into battle against their neighboring city states and by 1428 had formed a triple alliance with the towns of Tlacopan and Texcoco, gradually establishing their supremacy in the Valley of Mexico. As their empire expanded, they constructed impressive buildings and excelled in artistic accomplishments. They also introduced new educational systems.

Religion played an important part in the development of the arts. The Aztecs believed they lived in the "fifth world," the previous four having been destroyed by catastrophes. The most famous expression of their mythology is the impressive Stone of the Fifth Sun, commonly known as the Aztec Calendar. Discovered in Mexico City's Zócalo in 1790, it is displayed in the National

Right: mosaic of the Aztec calendar in Taxco

Above: Pyramid of the Sun, Teotihuacán

Museum of Anthropology in Mexico City (see pages 32–3).

Their foremost deities included Huitzilopochtli (their patron god), Tonatiuh (the sun god), Tezcatlipoca (the smoking mirror), and Quetzalcóatl (the plumed serpent). The Aztecs believed in appeasing their gods with human sacrifice, which they practiced on an even greater scale than previous civilizations.

They had a hierarchical social structure. The emperor, known as *tlatoani* (he who speaks), was not determined by heredity but was selected by a small group of electors, who became his council of advisors. Members of the

administration, judiciary, and army were called *tecuhtli*, and these posts were held for life. On a par with them were the priests, and also held in high esteem were craftsmen.

By the time Moctezuma II ascended the throne at the beginning of the 16th century, the Aztecs had developed into a rich and powerful empire with extensive dominions. Heavy taxes levied on neighboring states caused resentment and enmity, resulting in these groups joining the Spaniards in the eventual overthrow of the Aztec empire (see pages 14–15).

Pyramid of Quetzalcóatl, at Teotihuacán (left) and carving of his head on his temple (right)

Holy Places and Pyramids

This classic tour includes the Plaza of the Three Cultures, the Shrine of Guadalupe – the holiest place in Mexico – and the archaeological site at Teotihuacán. *A full day is recommended.*

Start from Alameda Central and take Paseo de la Reforma, travelling north. Turn left onto the Calzada Nonoalco to the Plaza de las Tres Culturas.

1 PLAZA DE LAS TRES CULTURAS

This square, in the city's northern district of Tlatelolco, features contrasting buildings from Mexico's three eras of history: pre-Columbian, Spanish colonial, and modern. The Aztec remains mark the spot of that people's final defeat by Cortés. The 17th-century Templo de Santiago in the middle

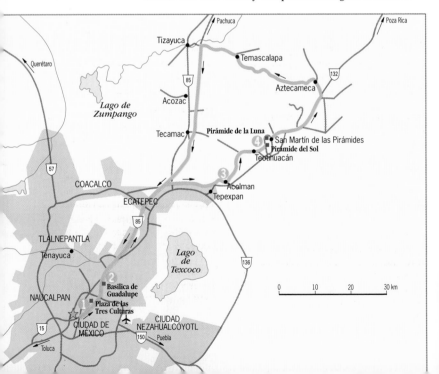

of the square is an example of Spanish architecture, and the tall building of the Foreign Ministry serves as a sharp contrast from the 20th century.
Rejoin Reforma and continue along the Calzada de Guadalupe to the Basílica.

2 BASÍLICA DE GUADALUPE
The original basilica has been replaced by this striking modern building, designed by Mexico's celebrated architect, Pedro Ramírez Vázquez. Consecrated in 1976, it is one of Latin America's most venerated shrines and Mexico's most important place of pilgrimage (see page 30). Pilgrims – some on their knees – make their way across the courtyard on the final stage of their journey. Inside, a moving walkway takes visitors slowly past the famous cloak bearing the image of the Virgin.
Take Insurgentes Norte (R85). Turn off east to Acolman.

3 MONASTERY OF ACOLMAN
This is a fine 16th-century Augustinian monastery, set in peaceful surroundings. Its façade is a good example of the plateresque style, while inside are some attractive murals and golden retables. The beautiful cloisters surround a small grove of orange trees.
Continue north for a short distance and follow the signs to San Juan Teotihuacán.

4 PYRAMIDS OF TEOTIHUACÁN
This ancient ceremonial center of pyramids, palaces, and broad avenues is positively grandiose (see page 67). While early structures are thought to date back to 100 BC, little is known of its origins. Teotihuacán's foremost deity was the rain god Tláloc, whose cult later merged with that of Quetzalcóatl, the plumed serpent.

At the southernmost entrance to the site, a small museum traces the history and development of Teotihuacán (there are *son et lumière* performances in the evenings, except for Mondays, subject to weather). The first structure, the Ciudadela (Citadel), centers around the Temple of Quetzalcóatl, noted for its sculptured serpents and masks. From here a broad street, the Avenue of the Dead, extends northwards for 4km, passing in front of the Pirámide del Sol, and ending at the Pirámide de la Luna. Designed and positioned with remarkable precision, they demonstrate the fullness of astronomical knowledge achieved by the Teotihuacanos. The climb up steps and platforms is rewarded with excellent views of the complex. The Pyramid of the Moon is much smaller than that of the Sun, but of equal height, being set on higher ground. Another structure of interest is the completely restored Palace of Quetzalpapálotl, part of the priests' residential complex.
Head for Tecamac and rejoin R85 to return to Mexico City.

TEOTIHUACÁN
The peak of the Teotihuacán culture was AD 300–600. It was a tightly run theocracy, in which the high priests controlled not only the religious but also the political and scientific life of the people. The place developed into a densely populated city, and exerted a far-reaching influence on many other religious centers spread over the vast México region. From the 8th century, there was a gradual decline, until the city was finally abandoned, five centuries before the Spaniards arrived.

To the Silver City

This is another popular tour from Mexico City, taking in flower-decked Cuernavaca, the stunningly pretty "Silver City" of Taxco, and the attractive spa resort of Ixtapan de la Sal, with wonderful mountain scenery included for good measure. *Allow a full day.*

Start from Reforma and take Insurgentes Sur south. Continue on toll highway 95 to Cuernavaca. This is a very pleasant route over the Ajusco Mountains, climbing up to a higher altitude before descending to Cuernavaca.

1 CUERNAVACA

With its pleasant climate, Cuernavaca has long been a favorite weekend retreat for residents of Mexico City. Now it is practically a suburb of the capital, with an increasing number of Mexicans (and foreigners) making it their permanent base,

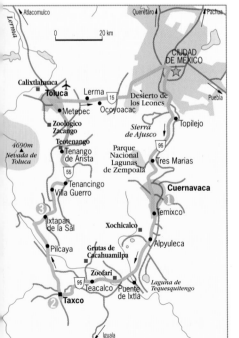

and the town is often choked with traffic. Known affectionately as the "City of Eternal Spring" for its agreeable climate, Cuernavaca is filled with brilliantly colored flowers. Bougainvillaea, oleanders, and jacarandas are seen in abundance adorning the houses and walled gardens.

Head for the center. The main square is charming, with plenty of flowers and greenery, the usual benches, and a bandstand in the center. On one side stands the elegant Governor's Palace. Opposite is a huge statue of Father Hidalgo's successor José María Morelos, one of the heroes of the War of Independence against Spain. Alongside is the Cuauhnáhuac Museum, formerly the Palace of Cortés. Here you can see a Diego Rivera mural depicting the Conquest of Mexico, along with many other paintings and sculptures.

A short walk leads to the cathedral.

This fortress-like structure, a former Franciscan church built in the 16th century, is set in an enclosed garden with chapels on either side. Its exterior could benefit from renovation, but the interior is a harmonious combination of original and modern elements. The cathedral is known for its *mariachi* Mass on Sundays.

Just beyond is the attractive Jardín Borda, with magnificent trees, fountains and a small boating lake, visited by Habsburg Emperor Maximilian and his wife Carlotta. If time permits, take a look at the Teopanzolco pyramid, near the railway station.

Continue on the R95 south to Taxco.

Woven rainbows make a warm souvenir of sunny days in Cuernavaca, Morelos

2 TAXCO

With its red-roofed, colonial-style houses clinging to the mountainside, Taxco always makes a delightful impression (see pages 66–7). Nestled in the mountains of the Sierra Madre, this is one of Mexico's most fascinating towns, and has long been designated a National Monument to preserve its colonial heritage. It is a pleasure to wander about the tiny cobblestone streets that wind their way steeply up the hillside (wear rubber-soled shoes for comfort and safety).

Mexico's "Silver City" prospered as a result of rich silver deposits mined in the 18th century. More recently it became renowned for the exquisite silverware

crafted here. The place is seriously tempting for shoppers, with beautiful silverware and handicrafts for sale everywhere (see pages 144–7).

The city's focal point is the pretty little tree-shaded main square, but its jewel is the Church of Santa Prisca, built of local pinkish stone. By the church are several flights of steps leading down to a daily market, where you will find bark paintings, wooden masks, and silver jewelry for sale.

Rejoin the R95. Take the R55 northwest to Ixtapan de la Sal.

3 IXTAPAN DE LA SAL

In complete contrast to the first two stops, the spa resort of Ixtapan de la Sal is a little oasis with cool green lawns, flowers, and fountains surrounded by forestland. There is a municipal spa and, on the outskirts, a privately run park with the full range of facilities. Luxurious hotels have pools and thermal baths in Greco-Roman style. The place tends to be lively on weekends.

Continue on the R55 to Toluca and take the R15 back to Mexico City.

Cuauhnáhuac Museum – open: Tuesday to Sunday 10am–5pm. Tel: 12–81–71. Admission charge.
Jardín Borda – open: Tuesday to Sunday 10am–5:30pm. Admission charge.
Santa Prisca Church – open: Monday to Saturday 7am–8pm, Sunday 6am–9pm.

Central Mexico and the Southern Gulf

*T*his area includes the central highlands around Mexico City, extending south to the state of Oaxaca, and eastward to the Gulf of Mexico. Within the region lies an enormous diversity of climates, landscapes, and cultures.

The central areas are characterized by great pine forests, lakes, and mountains. South of this the landscape is dominated by the snow-capped volcanoes that form the volcanic range extending from the Pacific coast to Veracruz on the Gulf of Mexico. This, in turn, gives way to the rugged mountains and valleys of Oaxaca, which contrast with the humid tropical jungles of the Gulf region.

This central region – the most populous area of Mexico and also of great economic importance – offers countless attractions. Three hundred years of Spanish rule resulted in delightful colonial towns, magnificent churches with elaborate interiors, charming old *haciendas* converted into hotels, and tranquil spa resorts. Surviving from an earlier era are numerous archaeological sites, vestiges of the Aztec, Toltec, and other pre-Columbian cultures.

Oaxaca, with its large indigenous populations, is known for its markets, pottery, and weaving. This region was once the center of the ancient Zapotec and Mixtec cultures. Monte Albán and Mitla are the most important of the pre-Hispanic sites in the area.

The cradle of Mexican civilization, however, is to be found in the Gulf basin, where the Olmecs developed the mother culture at La Venta. This is a region of dense jungle vegetation, tobacco, coffee and vanilla plantations, and tropical flowers.

Popocatépetl (Smoking Mountain) dominates the skyline at 5,452m: a path from the hut at Tlamacas leads to the summit

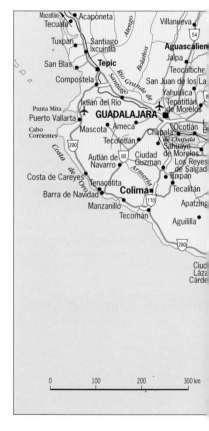

CENTRAL MEXICO AND THE SOUTHERN GULF

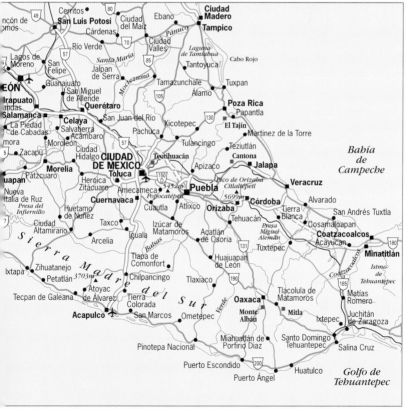

Walk the planks, down a wooden jetty, to choose your touring vessel at Lake Chapala

CHAPALA

This popular little resort town stands on the northern shores of Laguna de Chapala, the largest lake in Mexico. Its agreeable year-round climate is one of the factors that, for many years, have attracted foreign residents, especially from North America. Chapala – although close to Guadalajara, Mexico's second city – still maintains its tranquility.

The town has a pleasant promenade along the lakeshore, with lively bars and restaurants and *mariachi* musicians, who usually charge for their songs these days (part of the fun is to bargain and get a good deal). Launches are available for hire, as well as equipment for water sports. Along the lake to the west are the quaint little towns of Ajijic and Jocotepec, renowned for handicrafts and weaving.

42km south of Guadalajara. There are several daily bus services from the Central Camionera (Central Bus Station). The journey takes about 45 minutes.

CHOLULA

Legend claims that Cholula has a church for every day of the year. While the reality may fall well short of this, there are enough churches to serve a major metropolis. One of the most impressive is the 16th-century Franciscan San Gabriel church, on the zócalo. The Royal Chapel is remarkable for its huge atrium, once attended by great numbers of Indians. The zócalo itself is large and handsome. Cholula has been the location of the University of the Americas since 1970.

Most visitors come to see the great pyramid of Tepanapa, said to be the largest structure of its kind in the world (though not the tallest). It was once an important trading center and had religious ties with various cultures, from the Olmecs to the Aztecs. Guided tours can be taken to explore part of its vast network of tunnels. Crowning the site is the Spanish-built Church of Nuestra Señora de los Remedios.

Pyramid, Zona Arqueológica. Open: daily 10am–5pm. Admission charge (Sundays free).

12km west of Puebla, by bus, car, or taxi.

CUERNAVACA
See page 48.

EL TAJÍN
Lying northwest of Veracruz amid vanilla plantations bordering forested slopes, are the extensive ruins of El Tajín (which means "lightning" in Totonac). While its early origins are uncertain, some experts now attribute the city to the Huastecs, while others surmise the founders were of Maya lineage. It later developed as the ceremonial capital of the Totonacs, reaching its peak between AD 900 and 1100, when most of its finest buildings were erected. Later, the site was abandoned and lost to the jungle.

The site is dominated by the Pyramid of the Niches, a magnificent structure of six stories topped by a temple. A broad stairway runs up the main façade, while around the sides are 365 niches, tier upon tier, representing the days of the year. Two ball courts can be seen in this area, the south court having six detailed panels showing various rituals. A walk up the path leads to the Plaza of Tajín Chico, surrounded by another group of buildings. The Building of the Columns, which features great columns adorned with carvings, offers a fine view from the top, good for watching the dramatic spectacle of the "Flying Men of Papantla," who perform when there are sufficient numbers of tourists (see page 81).

20km southeast of Poza Rica. Open: Tuesday to Saturday 9am–6pm. Admission charge (Sundays free). By air from Mexico City to Poza Rica, then bus or taxi. Bus services from Mexico City to Poza Rica, leave from the Terminal Central Norte.

El Tajín's Pyramid of the God of Death (left), and the tiered Pyramid of the Niches (right)

GUADALAJARA

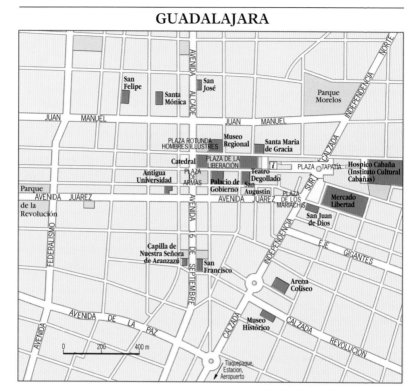

GUADALAJARA

Guadalajara is Mexico's second city, the capital of Jalisco state, and has a famously agreeable climate. It is a forward-looking, fast-developing metropolis that nevertheless retains its colonial heritage. The town center is one of parks and fountains, surrounded by mansions. The 16th-century, twin-towered Catedral is an impressive structure, flanked by four main squares arranged like a cross. Great works by José Clemente Orozco (1883–1949), one of Mexico's leading muralists, can be seen in the Palacio de Gobierno (Government Palace). More can be seen

in the central building of the University and the Instituto Cultural Cabañas cultural center, which houses the *Four Horsemen of the Apocalypse*. The splendid Teatro Degollado offers ballet, concerts, and folkloric shows.

Guadalajara is the home of the famous *mariachi* musicians; hear them at the Plaza de los Mariachis. The town is also the birthplace of the *charros*, Mexico's elegant rodeo riders.

In the surrounding areas *tequila* is produced, and the suburb of Tlaque-paque is a top crafts center (see page 147). *586km west of Mexico City. Information office: Sectur, Morelos 102, Plaza Tapatía.*

Tel: 614-01-23. Regular flights from Mexico City, other domestic destinations and the U.S. Rail and bus services from the north and Mexico City.

Catedral – open: daily 8am–7pm.
Instituto Cultural Cabañas – tel: 617–43–22. Open: Tuesday to Saturday 10.15am–6pm, Sunday 10.15am–3pm. Admission charge.
Palacio del Gobierno – Plaza de Armas. Open: weekdays 9am–6pm.
Teatro Degollado – Liberación Plaza. Tel: 614–47–73. Open: daily 10am–1pm, 4–7pm, and during performances.

GUANAJUATO

The old mining town of Guanajuato is one of Mexico's most appealing colonial towns, tucked away among a ring of hills in a spectacular setting. With beautiful old houses painted in many colors, crooked cobblestone streets winding up the hillsides, attractive squares, and unique subterranean streets, it is a town best explored on foot (see pages 68–9).

In the 1700s, Guanajuato was the prosperous center of a rich mining area. After silver was discovered in the surrounding hills, La Valenciana became one of the richest silver-producing mines in the world (and is still operative today).

Guanajuato was the first important town to be taken by the Mexicans in the Independence War. A local miner known as El Pípila reached the Alhóndiga de Granaditas (granary), where the Spaniards had taken refuge, and lost his life after setting its massive portals on fire. When Hidalgo and Allende, leaders of the movement, were captured and killed by the Spaniards, their heads were put on show in the granary until the end of the war. The place is now a museum. Just outside town is the catacomb-like Museo de las Momías, with dozens of excellently preserved mummies.

Guanajuato is home to one of Mexico's foremost universities. Strolling musicians from the university, known as *estudiantinas*, add to the lively atmosphere. The Teatro Juárez stages plays, concerts, and cultural events year round, while the famed Cervantino Festival takes place here each October (see page 154). This is also the birthplace of renowned muralist Diego Rivera. His former home is now a museum.

A ride up San Miguel Hill, to the gigantic El Pípila monument offers a magnificent view of the town. The nearby Valenciana church is a stunning Churrigueresque building, and the famous mine is across the road. Another trip of interest is to the colossal *Christ the King* figure on Cubilete Hill, considered Mexico's geographical center.

376km northwest of Mexico City. Information office: Sectur, Plaza de la Paz. Tel: 2–00–86. Flights from Mexico City and U.S. destinations. Bus and rail services from Mexico City and other towns.

Alhóndiga de Granaditas – Calle de 28 de Septiembre. Tel: 2–11–12. Open: Tuesday to Saturday 10am–2pm, 4–6pm; Sunday 10am–4pm. Admission charge.
Museo de las Momías – Panteón Municipal. Tel: 2–06–39. Open: Tuesday to Sunday 10am–6pm. Admission charge.
Museo Diego Rivera Museum – Pocitos 47. Tel: 2–11–97. Open: Tuesday to Saturday 10am–1.30pm, 4–6.30pm; Sunday 10am–2.30pm. Admission charge.

Mitla

One of the foremost archaeological sites in the state of Oaxaca, Mitla belongs to the Zapotec and Mixtec civilizations, and is renowned for its magnificent mosaic work adorning the buildings (attributed to the Mixtecs). The site is just off the main square of the tiny village of Mitla, which bustles with stalls and vendors selling colorful traditional clothes, woven rugs, basketware, and local handicrafts. The Museo Frissell de Arte Zapoteca (Frissell Museum), also just off the main square, has a fine collection of Zapotec and Mixtec artifacts (open: daily 9am–6pm; free).

Mitla's first inhabitants were the Zapotecs, and by the 1st century AD it had become an important religious center. Around the 10th century, the Mixtecs arrived from the central region of Mexico, and their culture reached its peak in the 13th century. Mitla gets its name from a Náhuatl word meaning "Place of the Dead," for the burial grounds there, but it has also inherited the name "Place of Palaces" for its masterfully ornamented buildings. This was the work of the Mixtecs, known as

the "Cloud People." Skilled artisans, they produced beautiful structures covered with fine ornamentation and mosaics, set in geometric patterns of coils and keys to depict a stylized plumed serpent – among other religious symbols.

Unlike many other archaeological sites that have been uncovered, Mitla stands largely intact and relatively little restoration has been necessary. It covers a fairly small area, and is divided into five groups, of which only two have been fully excavated.

The most important is the Grupo de las Columnas, a group of columns built around two patios. The Salón de las

The remains of a Mixtec mosaic design show an aesthetic sense of classic sophistication

OTHER ARCHAEOLOGICAL SITES
Between Mitla and Oaxaca are
several smaller Zapotec sites. Near
Mitla are the Zapotec ruins of Yagul
(Old Hill). The major structure is the
Palacio de los Seis Patios (Palace of
the Six Courtyards). Nearer Oaxaca
are the sites of Dainzú, which is only
partially excavated, and Lambityeco.
Yagul – open: daily 8am–6pm.
Lambityeco – open: daily 8am–5pm.
Dainzú – open: daily 8am–6pm.
Small admission charge for each site
(Sundays free).

Columnas features six large columns;
from here a narrow passageway leads to
the Patio de las Grecas, also known as
the Fret Patio on account of the
geometric patterns on the walls. This is
the highlight of the site, displaying the
exquisite workmanship of the Mixtec
artisans, who used thousands of cut
stones to make up the mosaic pattern.

In front of the complex is the
entrance to an underground tomb, also
decorated with mosaics. The Columna
de la Vida (Column of Life) in front of
the entrance is supposed to measure life
expectancy, as calculated by the distance
left after placing your arms around the
column.

Second in importance is the Grupo de
la Iglesia (Church Group), which also
features richly adorned buildings. Other
buildings include the Grupo del Sur
(South Group), and to the west the
Grupo del Arroyo (Arroyo Group) and
the Grupo de los Adobos (Adobe
Group).
*Mitla ruins – open: 8am–5pm. Admission
charge (Sundays and holidays free).*

Mitla's tourist market (above); El Tule
(below), already old at the time of Christ

*38km southeast of Oaxaca. Most people
take a tour from Oaxaca. This usually
includes a stop to admire the Tule Tree.
This extraordinary giant ahuehuete has a
circumference of 57m (the largest in the
world) and is believed to be about 2,500
years old.*

Monte Albán

*M*onte Albán (White Mountain) is Oaxaca's top attraction. Built on a flat hilltop with a spectacular view of the mountains and broad valley of Oaxaca, this is one of Mexico's foremost archaeological sites and a major testimony to the Zapotec and Mixtec civilizations.

Monte Albán's origins are not known, although there is evidence to suggest influences of the Olmecs' La Venta culture. Between about 600 BC and AD 1200, it was developed in distinct stages by the Zapotecs, and it grew to become an important religious center with a population peaking at 25,000. After this time, Monte Albán fell into decline and was gradually abandoned by the Zapotecs. Around AD 1300, the place was taken over by the Mixtecs, who used it as burial grounds for their dignitaries.

A path up the hillside from the parking lot leads to the entrance, which is on the northeast corner. Here you will be met by the grandeur of the Gran Plaza, a vast grassy area surrounded by great solid structures, with a group of buildings in the center. Stairways and platforms enable you to scramble up and down the temples with ease.

Down on your left is the ball court; no stone rings can be seen, as with other ball courts in the Oaxaca region. Over to your right is the impressive Plataforma Norte (North Platform), which offers a magnificent view from the top. Continuing counter-clockwise, you will pass another monument known simply as Sistema IV (System IV), before arriving at one of the most interesting sections of the complex. Los Danzantes (The Dancers) are a set of stelae with figures carved in strange dance-like positions. There are many differing theories as to the significance of these figures, which show deformities and – judging by their features – a strong Olmec influence.

At the far end of the Gran Plaza is the Plataforma Sur (South Platform), largest of the structures. A climb to the top of the platform will give you an excellent view of the site and its surrounding hills.

From here, you can walk across to the central buildings. The arrow-shaped

An intriguing detail of *The Dancers*, showing one of the variously interpreted carvings

The view north from the South Platform over the Zapotec ruins and the Gran Plaza

BALL GAMES

To the peoples of pre-Conquest Mexico, the innocent-sounding ball game (known as *tlachtli*) was both a religious ritual and a form of recreation in which spectators would gamble on the outcome. The ball, of solid rubber, was kept in constant motion in the air by the players using only their hips, elbows, or knees, mimicking the movements of the heavenly bodies, and perhaps itself symbolizing the sun or moon. The players may also have tried to re-enact victorious battles. The finale was frequently a gruesome human sacrifice: either the loser was decapitated and his head possibly used as a ball, or he was tortured to death and his body trussed up into a ball shape by the victor and bounced down the steps of the pyramid.

Montículo (Mound) is one of the earliest and most complex structures to be found here. Adjacent to it is another group known as Edificios (Buildings) G, H, and I. To your right is the building known as El Palacio (The Palace), where a passageway leads to an impressive patio, indicating that the temple may have been used to house dignitaries.

Of interest, too, are the tombs located beyond the North Platform. In 1932, priceless treasures were found in some of these, especially Tombs 7 and 104, which can be seen in Oaxaca's Regional State Museum. Archaeologist Dr. Alfonso Caso, honored by a monument at the entrance, discovered some 50 tombs here during the course of his work.

6km west of Oaxaca. Open: daily 8am–5pm. Admission charge (Sundays and holidays free). Best visited by tour from Oaxaca.

The jewel of Oaxaca, the interior of the exquisite church of Santo Domingo

OAXACA

The clarity of its skies and its Valley of Mexico setting, surrounded by mountains, give the state capital a special attraction. With its churches, museums, handicrafts, markets, and ambience, Oaxaca combines colonial architecture with an indigenous population. It also serves as a base for excursions to major ruins and colorful Indian markets in the region.

The zócalo (see page 70) is the focal point of life in Oaxaca. Closed to traffic, it has neat trees, inviting benches, and an elegant bandstand where rousing concerts are held, all surrounded by arcades and cafés. Sunday is especially enjoyable, with Indian women weaving and selling their wares. The Mercado de Abastos is Oaxaca's famed daily market. Located on the southwestern outskirts of town, it is at its liveliest and most colorful on Saturdays.

On the north side of the zócalo stands the Catedral. Started in 1533 and completed 200 years later, it has a fine baroque façade of greenish stone and a clock donated by the King of Spain. A few blocks away is Oaxaca's most impressive church, the 16th-century

Templo de Santo Domingo (see page 70). Its rich interior, gilded and painted by Mexican craftsmen, is one of the most significant in the country. Not far from here is the Basílica de la Soledad, with a jewel-encrusted statue of the Virgin.

Housed in the monastery of Santo Domingo, the Museo Regional de Oaxaca (see page 71) has a rich collection of artifacts, including treasures

Basílica de la Soledad – Avenida de la Independencia. Open: daily 5:30am–9pm.
Museo Regional de Oaxaca – tel: 6–29–91. Open: Tuesday to Friday 10am–6pm; weekends 10am–5pm. Admission charge.
Museo Rufino Tamayo – Avenida Morelos. Tel: 6–47–50. Open: Monday and Wednesday to Saturday 10am–2pm, 4–7pm; Sunday 10am–3pm. Admission charge.
Templo de Santo Domingo – Calle Macedonio Alcalá and Calle A Gurrión. Open: daily 7am–8pm.

from the tombs of Monte Albán. The
nearby Museo Rufino Tamayo (see page
71) has a fine collection of pre-
Columbian works donated by the
renowned local artist.
*523km southeast of Mexico City. Tourist
office: 5 de Mayo and Avenida Morelos.
Tel: 6–48–28. Frequent flights from Mexico
City and other towns. Regular bus
connections to the capital and other centers.*

ORIZABA
Orizaba makes an attractive stop on the
way to the city of Veracruz, mainly for its
lush setting with stunning views of Pico
de Orizaba, Mexico's highest volcano.
*276km southeast of Mexico City. Regular
bus from Mexico City and Veracruz.*

PÁTZCUARO
This quaint little town in the west of
Mexico's central region is the heartland
of the Tarascan Indians. Fishing,
farming, and handicrafts are the main
means of livelihood.

The town is one of cobblestone
streets and red-roofed houses. Its most
attractive feature is the park-like Plaza
Principal Vasco de Quiroga, with a
fountain, ash trees, and handsome
buildings surrounding it. Places of
interest include the Casa del Gigante
(House of the Giant) on the square and
the small shopping center of Casa de los
Once Patios (House of Eleven Patios).
The Museo de Artes Populares, housed
in the former Colegio de San Nicolás,
displays masks, textiles, local pottery,
copper, lacquerware, and straw figures.
One block north of the Museum of
Popular Art, the Basílica de Nuestra
Señora de la Salud (Our Lady of Health)
– started in 1554 and rebuilt in 1883 –
contains a celebrated cornpaste image of
the Virgin.

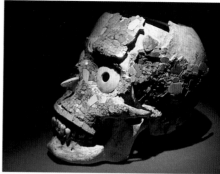

Pre-Columbian artifact, Rufino Tamayo Museum

Many visitors make the trip to nearby
Lake Pátzcuaro – 10 minutes by bus or
taxi to the jetty. Restaurants line the
marina and boats can take you across to
Janitzio (a 40-minute journey). This tiny
island rises up like a cone, with
picturesque little houses and terraced
steps leading up to a gigantic statue of
Morelos, hero of the War of
Independence. Janitzio is rustic and
crammed with restaurants, stalls, and
handicraft shops all the way up. The
climb is steep, but worth it for the view.

The "butterfly net" style of fishing,
once a big attraction, is rarely used now,
except by request. Janitzio is famed for
its Festival of the Day of the Dead (see
page 155).
*Pátzcuaro is 365km west of Mexico City.
There are bus services from Morelia and
other destinations.*

**Basílica de Nuestra Señora de la
Salud** – Calle Lerín.
Museo de Artes Populares – Calle
Lerín. Open: Tuesday to Saturday
9am–7pm, Sunday 9am–3pm.
Admission charge.

The Rosary Chapel takes pride of place at the church of Santo Domingo, Puebla

PUEBLA

Watched over by four snow-topped volcanoes – Orizaba, Popocatépetl, Iztaccíhuatl, and the smaller La Malinche – Puebla is Mexico's fourth largest town and a thriving commercial center. The town was laid out by the Spaniards, who introduced the art of tile-making, and its churches and façades, adorned with Talavera tiles, speak eloquently of those colonial days.

Puebla has many fine churches. The vast cathedral (see page 72), located on the south side of the main square, is considered one of the most important in Mexico. Built between the mid-16th and 18th centuries, it has a rather austere Renaissance-style façade, a tiled dome, gorgeous carving in the choir, and some 14 chapels. Nearby, the 17th-century Templo de Santo Domingo (see page 72) is noted for its Capilla del Rosario (Rosary Chapel), one of Mexico's masterpieces. Museo Amparo, noted for its fine collection of pre-Hispanic and colonial art; the Archbishop's Palace which contains the Biblioteca Palafoxiana (Palafox Library) and the Casa de Cultura; and the richly tiled Casa del Alfeñique (Sugarcake House). Serving as Puebla's regional museum, it features archaelogical artifacts, historical relics, and regional crafts.

Lying 97km east of Puebla is the newly excavated site of Cantona, which is believed to have developed during the 8th century AD. Built into the hillside, it covers a large area containing ceremonial structures and numerous ballcourts. *126km southeast of Mexico City. Tourist office: 5 Oriente No. 3. Tel: 46–12–85. There are frequent buses from Mexico City and other centers.*

Catedral – open: 6am–noon, 4:30–8pm.
Biblioteca Palafoxiana – open: Tuesday to Sunday 10am–5pm. Admission charge.
Museo Regional – Avenida 4 Oriente 418. Open: Tuesday to Sunday 10am–5pm. Admission charge.
Templo de Santo Domingo – open: 7:30am–8pm.
Museo Amparo – open: Wednesday to Monday 10am–5pm. Charge.

QUERÉTARO

Querétaro is often bypassed by visitors in their rush to reach the more obvious attractions of Guanajuato and San Miguel de Allende. But within its industrial outskirts lies a historic town with a colonial center, small plazas, fine stone buildings, and intricate wrought-iron work. It features an old aqueduct, and is known for its opals and semi-precious stones.

Main squares are the Plaza de Armas, Jardín Obregón, and the Jardín de la Corregidora, where a statue honors "La Corregidora," Josefa Ortíz de Domínguez, who warned Father Hidalgo and the other conspirators plotting against Spain of their imminent arrest. Churches and buildings of interest include the Templo de Santa Rosa de Viterbo, the Templo de Santa Clara, and the Museo Regional, which is housed in the old 17th-century Franciscan monastery.

A short trip northwest of the center takes you to the Cerro de las Campanas (Hill of Bells), where a flight of steps set in attractive gardens leads up to a tiny chapel. This marks the spot of Emperor Maximilian's execution by firing squad. On the brow of the hill stands a huge, menacing statue of the man who ordered his death, Benito Juárez.

213km north of Mexico City. Tourist office: Pasteur 4 Norte, Plaza Independencia. Tel: 12–14–12. There are bus and rail services from Mexico City and other destinations.

> **Museo Regional** – Corregidora 3 Sur, Tel: 12–20–31. Open: Tuesday to Sunday 10am–4pm. Admission charge.

SAN MIGUEL DE ALLENDE

This little town is a National Monument and a real gem, with steep cobblestone streets, hidden courtyards, and a magnificent church. It is dominated by the Iglesia Parroquial (parish church), a huge 19th-century neo-gothic structure in pink stone. Below it, surrounded by arcades, is the pretty little zócalo with neatly trimmed trees and benches. The center is compact and filled with art

galleries, boutiques, and handicrafts, for which the town is renowned. The Instituto Allende is a well-established art center, housed in a beautiful old 18th-century mansion.

286km north of Mexico City. Tourist office: on Plaza de Allende. Tel: 2–17–47. Buses from Mexico City and other centers.

A lovely *señorita* sits on a gracious bench in the zócalo of San Miguel de Allende

> **Iglesia Parroquial** – Plaza de Allende. Open: Tuesday to Saturday 10am–4pm, Sunday 10am–2pm.
> **Instituto Allende** – Calzada Ancho de San Antonio. Tel: 2–01–90. Open: Monday to Friday 9am–6pm, Saturday 9am–1pm.

SILVER MINING

The Spaniards who conquered
Mexico in 1521 lusted after the gold
of the Aztecs. Although initial
explorations were disappointing, it was
not long before rich veins of a different
precious metal were discovered in the
mountainous regions of Zacatecas,
Guanajuato, and Pachuca.

Silver mining started to develop in
a big way. Zacatecas gradually became
more prosperous until, by the
beginning of the 17th
century, it was one
of the richest cities
in Mexico. Silver also
brought wealth to
Guanajuato. The
Valenciana Mine,
established in 1766,
became one of the
world's most productive
silver mines.Taxco, too,
prospered after large

Left to right: Taxco
silversmith; tools
from La Valenciana;
El Pedgreal silver
mine, Taxco; silver
artifacts, both
beautiful and
functional

become the world's top producer of silver by the end of the 17th century.

Enforced Indian labor was used for working the mines, and living and working conditions for these miners were very tough. Later, legislation improved matters and unions were formed.

Over time, however, gradual decline set in, mines closed down, and some old mining centers were abandoned to become ghost towns. Others, like the Valenciana Mine of Guanajuato, have been reactivated and continue in operation today. El Solar is one of several productive silver mines functioning around Taxco, where the town's flourishing silver industry earned it the nickname of "Silver City." Hundreds of shops there display exquisitely wrought silverware and jewelry. Once again, Mexico ranks as the world's foremost producer of silver.

deposits of silver were discovered nearby in the mid-18th century by Frenchman José de la Borda.

The vast amounts of silver, gold, and other minerals shipped to Spain made an important contribution to its economy. After a fall in silver output in the mid-1660s, Mexico recovered to

TAXCO

The beauty of Taxco is legendary (see pages 48–9). Long declared a National Monument, the town's old buildings are preserved and new construction is limited to colonial style. Whitewashed houses with red-tiled roofs spread up the mountainsides in an enchanting setting.

Although silver had already been discovered earlier by the Spaniards, Taxco was literally put on the map in the early 1800s, when French prospector and miner José de la Borda found a series of rich silver veins in the area. While accruing his own fortune, he also sponsored the construction of the superb church of Santa Prisca.

The silver industry had declined, however, when a New Orleans professor of architecture, Bill Spratling, came to Taxco in 1929 to write a book and fell in

love with the place. He trained the locals in silversmithing, thus preventing the demise of the town, and this developed into a profitable business. Taxco is now synonymous with silver.

This is a delightful place in which to wander around (wear rubber-soled shoes to cope with the cobblestones). The outstanding pink stone Santa Prisca church would be worth a detour on its own merits alone. Behind, down a series of steps, is the local market. Nearby is the Spratling Museum, with a historical survey of Taxco and pre-Columbian pieces. For a stunning view, take a cable car up to the Monte Taxco Hotel, high over the hills. To visit El Solar silver mine on the outskirts of town, an appointment is needed (tel: 2–03–94). *164km south of Mexico City. Tourist office: Avenida de los Plateros. Tel: 2–15–25. Regular bus services from Mexico City and Acapulco.*

A view of Taxco from El Indito restaurant

Spratling Museum – Porfirio
Delgado and El Arco. Tel: 2–16–60.
Open: Tuesday to Saturday
10am–5pm, Sunday 9am–3pm.
Admission charge.

TEOTIHUACÁN

Teotihuacán was the first known urban civilization in Mesoamerica and by the 4th century AD it had become the greatest power in the area. But when the Aztecs arrived in the Valley of Mexico in the 12th century, it had long been abandoned (see pages 46–7). Only the city's art and architecture offer clues to their way of life. The most significant phase of development began in the 2nd century BC. By the 1st century AD, massive pyramids and temples testified to its importance as a religious and political center. The second phase (*c* AD 200–350) was one of conquest and continued building. In its final phase (*c* 350–450) it reached its greatest splendor and dominated an area of some 20sq km, with a population estimated at 200,000.

Open: daily 8am–5pm. Son et lumière October to March (7pm in English).

VERACRUZ

Mexico's principal seaport is also its oldest. It was here, on Good Friday in 1519, that Hernán Cortés arrived on the first stage of the Spanish Conquest. He planted a cross (for which the settlement was named), and the place became an important trading port with Europe. Later, French and American troops landed here during various conflicts.

Veracruz is one of the liveliest towns in Mexico, with an interesting mix of Mexican and Afro-Caribbean people. The main square, the Plaza de las Armas, is the scene of strolling musicians and never-ending activity. The town is famous for its *jarocho* music and colorful Shrovetide Carnival.

The latest attraction is the new giant Acuario (Aquarium), impressive both in size and content.

The extended *malecón* (waterfront promenade) offers a pleasant walk along the busy harbor. Across the bay is the 16th-century island fortress of San Juan de Ulúa. Formerly a fort and prison, it now houses a small regional museum.

South of town, Boca del Río has excellent open-air seafood restaurants. Lake Mandinga, beyond, offers boat trips through the mangroves, and you will also find good seafood served along the lake.
427km east of Mexico City. Tourist office: Palacio Municipal. Tel: 32–19–99/99–42. Regular flights from Mexico City. Bus and rail services.

A copy of the *Marigallante*, in Veracruz harbor

San Juan de Ulúa – open: Tuesday to Sunday 9am–5pm. Admission charge (Sundays free).

Guanajuato

For this walk through the cultural heart of beautiful colonial Guanajuato (see page 55), wear comfortable shoes for the cobblestone streets and watch out for busy traffic. *Allow 3 hours.*

Start in the Plaza Dr. Romero. Take a look at the fine façade of the 18th-century Templo de San Francisco (Church of St. Francis), and walk up the left side of the Calle Sopena to the museum.

1 MUSEO ICONOGRÁFICO DEL QUIJOTE

This extraordinary Iconographic Museum of Don Quixote, opened in 1987, has a collection of almost 600 works relating to Miguel Cervantes's famous character, donated by the Spaniard Señor Eulalio Ferrier. Its many rooms contain paintings, lithographs, and sculptures of this famous man of fiction, including works by Picasso and Dalí (open Tuesday to

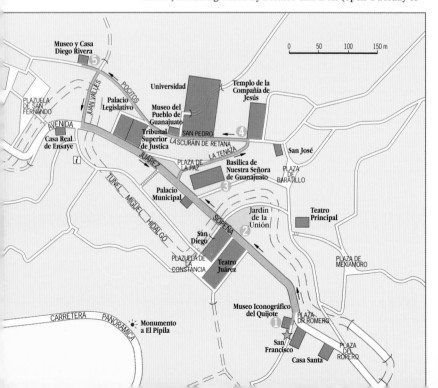

Saturday 10am–6:30pm, Sunday 10am–2:30pm; closed Monday; admission charge).

Continue up Calle Sopena. On your left you will pass the splendid Teatro Juárez (Juárez Theater), followed by the Templo de San Diego (St. James's Church). Behind is the Casa de las Artesanías (Arts and Crafts Center). Continue up to Jardín de la Unión.

2 JARDÍN DE LA UNIÓN

Union Garden is a lovely square, a focal point with laurel trees, benches, cafés, and restaurants lining the far side. It is always lively, a favorite meeting place for locals and students. In the evenings, musicians try their luck.

Proceed up to the Plaza de la Paz to the Basílica.

3 BASÍLICA DE NUESTRA SEÑORA DE GUANAJUATO

Our Lady of Guanajuato is a 17th-century baroque basílica, standing imposingly up a flight of steps. Inside is a much revered statue of the Virgin, donated in 1557 by King Philip II of Spain.

Go around to the left of the Basílica and down La Tenaza to the Jesuit Church.

4 TEMPLO DE LA COMPAÑÍA DE JESÚS

This 18th-century Jesuit Church, which holds a commanding position on a hilltop, is noted for its magnificent Churrigueresque façade in pink stone. The somewhat austere interior features a red-brick ceiling, Guanajuato-style, and statues of saints in the niches.

Turn right from the church and walk up Calle San Pedro Lascuráin de Retana. On your right pass an impressive flight of steps leading up to the Universidad (University) of Guanajuato. On your left are cafés, bars,

The Jesuit Church façade is an example of the highly ornate Churrigueresque style

and restaurants. Continue along Calle Pocitos, passing the local Museo del Pueblo de Guanajuato to a Venetian red house marked no. 47, which is the Museo y Casa de Diego Rivera.

5 MUSEO CASA DIEGO RIVERA

Mexico's great muralist was born in this house in 1886, and lived here as a child. Furniture and old photographs offer a glimpse of everyday life in the last century. As well as some of his works and sketches, there are sculptures and exhibits of other artists (open: Tuesday to Saturday 10am–1.30pm, 4–6.30pm, Sunday 10am–2.30pm; closed Monday; admission charge. Tel: 2–11–97).

Turn left back down Pocitos, right down Calle Juan Valles, then left, passing the splendid Palacio Legislativo on your left. There are shops on your right. Finish with a drink at the Plaza de la Paz.

Oaxaca

Oaxaca is a town for leisurely strolling. This walk through the center includes a look at its major colonial attractions, combined with the flavor of its indigenous population (see pages 60–1). *Allow 3 hours.*

Start at the zócalo (main square).

1 ZÓCALO

This beautiful square, surrounded by arcades, is the hub of Oaxaca and a marvelous place for lingering in one of the many cafés and restaurants, watching the nonstop activity: local women with long dark plaits and colorful costumes, the ubiquitous vendors, musicians coming and going. The square leads into an adjoining square that is dominated on its northern side by the cathedral.

Pass by the Catedral, turn right along Avenida Independencia, cross over and take Calle Macedonia Alcalá, a pedestrian street with houses painted in different colors, a few shops, and markets. You will pass the Casa de Cortés, which now houses the city museum. Continue to the Plaza Santo Domingo on your right.

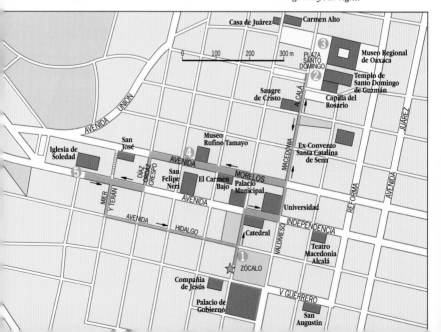

If it's edible or usable, it's here in Oaxaca's colorful Benito Juárez market

2 TEMPLO DE SANTO DOMINGO DE GUZMÁN

On this large open plaza, adorned by striking flamboyant trees, stands St. Dominic's Church. Founded in the late 16th century, its vaulted ceiling is inset with 36 paintings by local craftspeople. Of special note is the genealogical tree of the Guzmáns, the family of Domingo de Guzmán, 13th-century founder of the Dominican Order.

Adjoining is the Museo Regional de Oaxaca.

3 MUSEO REGIONAL DE OAXACA

Housed in the former monastery (Ex-Convento) of Santo Domingo, Oaxaca's regional museum is a beautiful building of grand cloisters, and worth seeing in itself. The fine collection includes artifacts from the Zapotec and Mixtec cultures. Outstanding are the objects of gold, crystal, and other materials found in Tomb 7 in Monte Albán, displayed in a special room on the left as you enter.

Nearby are some attractive shops. Across from the museum, the Palacio de Santo Domingo shopping center offers a wide variety of colorful handicrafts, and

in the Oro de Monte Albán you can buy beautifully made reproductions of the Mixtec gold jewelry from Tomb 7. You can also watch goldsmiths at work.

Return down Macedonia Alcalá and turn right along Avenida Morelos to the Museo Rufino Tamayo.

4 MUSEO RUFINO TAMAYO

Rufino Tamayo was a native of Oaxaca, and is considered one of Mexico's great artists. He died in 1991. This lovely old colonial mansion contains a collection of pre-Columbian and other pieces from his private collection.

Take Díaz Ordáz Crespo and turn right along Avenida Independencia to the Basílica de la Soledad.

5 BASÍLICA DE LA SOLEDAD

This is another of Oaxaca's lovely churches, built in the 17th century. Inside is the graceful figure of Our Lady of Solitude, the city's patron saint. Notable is the vast gold crown adorned with diamonds. Behind the church is a small museum devoted to the Virgin.

Turn down Mier Y Teran, left onto Avenida Hidalgo, and back to the zócalo.

The Route of the Churches

This tour in and around Puebla takes you to some of Mexico's most interesting and unusual churches, examples that combine the best of colonial and Indian skills and artistic vision (see page 62). *Allow 3 hours.*

Start in the main square, Plaza de la Constitución, and walk over to the cathedral on the south side.

1 CATEDRAL

This vast structure, the second largest in Mexico, has a rather austere look. Started in 1575, it took 100 years to complete. Relief figures on the north doorway depict the four Spanish Habsburg Kings – Charles V and Philips II, III, and IV. The style is part baroque, part Renaissance.

Cross the lively zócalo and take the ramblas, Cinco de Mayo, on the other side to the Templo de Santo Domingo on the left.

2 TEMPLO DE SANTO DOMINGO

St. Dominic's Church dates back to the early 17th century and has a baroque façade. Inside is a veritable jewel, the Capilla del Rosario (Rosary Chapel), gloriously decorated with gold leaf and sculptures. On a Sunday, you might well come across a christening or some other local event.

Now walk back towards the main square and take a taxi for a little tour of the surroundings. Agree on a price, usually calculated by the

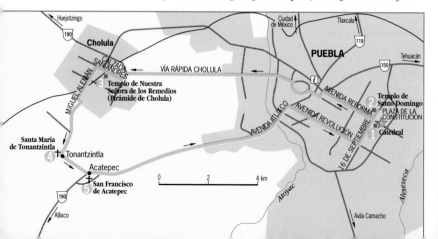

hour. It takes about 15 minutes to the pyramid and church of Cholula.

3 PIRÁMIDE DE CHOLULA AND TEMPLO DE NUESTRA SEÑORA DE LOS REMEDIOS

Here you will find the largest pyramid in the world in terms of circumference, topped by a charming little church with twin yellow towers. The pyramid dates back to before the Classic period of pre-Hispanic Mexico, and is believed to have been built over seven times. To visit the tunnels inside (where a small flashlight is useful), you must buy a ticket at the ticket window across the road. There is a children's playground in front, and a single railway track alongside. You can climb up to the church, which was built by the Spaniards in 1666, and rebuilt in the mid-19th century after it was damaged by an earthquake. Inside is a Madonna in a glass case, said to have been presented by Cortés. There are wonderful views from both this spot and the hill opposite; with a magnificent backdrop provided by the snowy peak of the Orizaba volcano.

Continue to the church of Santa María de Tonantzintla, located a few kilometers southwest, just outside the tiny village of the same name.

4 SANTA MARÍA DE TONANTZINTLA

This enchanting church was constructed in the 18th century entirely by local Indians. The appealing exterior consists of a single tower, red and blue tiles, and honey-colored side walls. The interior is delightful, with every inch covered by exuberant decorations of cherubs, fruit, and other patterns.

About 2km farther along is the Church of San Francisco de Acatepec.

5 SAN FRANCISCO DE ACATEPEC

This is another beauty. More sumptuous than the previous church, it has a magnificent façade tiled in typical *poblano* (Puebla) style in red, blue, and yellow, with twin towers. The interior which was also partly the work of Indians, is richly decorated, with an elaborate gilded altar.

Return to Puebla, 5km east.

Santo Domingo's gorgeous Rosary Chapel is fitting of a nation devoted to the Virgin

Pirámide de Cholula and church – open: daily 10am–5pm. Admission charge.

A Climb Up Popocatépetl

This climb reaches the snowy summit of the 5,452m volcano of Popocatépetl. The best time to go is mid-November to mid-March, although this can vary from year to year. Though not exceptionally difficult, the ascent is long and strenuous and climbers must be in optimum condition. *This climb is by the normal route via Las Cruces and takes from 6 to 8 hours to reach the top, plus 3 hours to descend. You can hire a guide at Tlamacas, or undertake it yourself.*

Start from the Tlamacas hut (altitude approximately 3,960m), which can be reached from Mexico City by bus via Amecameca (2 to 3 hours). You must arrive the previous evening to start the climb between 2am and 4am in the morning.

PREPARATIONS

Tlamacas has a large hut with sleeping facilities, but bring your own food. For the climb, you will need ski-poles or an ice-axe, depending on snow conditions, crampons, a head lamp for the early departure, climbing boots, and provisions for emergencies (equipment can be rented).
This first stage will take around 2 hours.

Popocatépetl as seen from the national park that surrounds it

1 STAGE ONE

Setting off in the dark, you start the ascent over a lava sand path that rises immediately behind the hut in the direction of Las Cruces. At the first fork, take the wide path to the left (not the steep one to the right, which leads to a more difficult route) and stay on this path. After one and a half hours, the lava path divides. Turn right on to a fairly wide trail (not the dirt track to the left), which climbs very steeply to Las Cruces, where there used to be a hut. This section takes about 45 minutes and should be taken carefully and slowly.
Do not try to break records. Take it easy. You still have 1,000m to the summit. The next stage takes about 3 to 4 hours.

2 LAS CRUCES TO THE CRATER

Now comes the real climb. Behind the remnants of the base, the way leads steeply up lava dust to the snowline. Depending on weather conditions, keep more to the left. The red markings on the rock ends indicate short cuts, but climbers who are not fully adjusted to the climate would be better advised to stick to the normal route. After about an hour, the gradient to the far left is crossed in an easterly direction towards the crater. Larger or smaller serpentines are necessary depending on the weather. Some 50m below the rim of the crater, the normal route passes by a large imposing rock to the lower rim of the crater, the Labio Inferior.
To get this far is a triumph in itself!

3 THE CRATER

At 5, 252m above sea level, this is considered to be virtually a summit victory. The crater has a depth of 480m and rim-to-rim distances of 850m by 750m, and it still belches clouds of sulphur. Do not attempt to descend into the crater, as there is a risk of suffocation.
It is only another hour or so from here to the summit.

4 UP TO THE SUMMIT

Follow a direct route along the crater rim towards the summit. After the rocks, turn approximately 10m into the northeast glacier and then return to the rim. Reaching the summit, Pico Major, gives you a feeling of great elation. Subject to weather and smog, you will have unrivalled views of Mexico City, Iztaccíhuatl, Puebla, and, away in the distance, Pico de Orizaba.
Now comes the descent, which should take about 3 hours.

5 THE DESCENT

The descent is quite steep and you must take great care, particularly when you reach the lava beds, where you can run the risk of sliding.
You can stay overnight in Tlamacas to shower and relax, or return to Mexico City the same evening.

PRECAUTIONS

Altitude sickness can affect anyone – symptoms include nausea, severe headaches, light-headedness, disorientation, and dizziness. If you suffer from any of these, stop and rest. Should it appear more serious, descend and, if necessary, seek medical help. A day spent at Tlamacas beforehand can help you to acclimatize.
N.B. With eruptions of Popocatépetl still occurring, climbers should check with the authorities for latest developments.

The Pacific Coast

*M*exico's Pacific coastline stretches over 7,000km, from the country's northwest corner, where it meets California, down to its southern border with Guatemala. The slopes and valleys of the great Sierra Madre Occidental, which parallels the west coast, provide a lush green backdrop to much of the coastal scenery. In the southern regions, there are large, thriving plantations of bananas, mangoes, and coconuts. The whole coast is punctuated with beautiful bays ringed by mountains and long stretches of sandy beaches, broken up by rock formations.

Until the 1920s, the coast supported only a handful of small towns and tiny isolated fishing villages. But as more roads were built, tourism became possible. It started with Acapulco, which has long been internationally famous. Other resorts followed. Puerto Vallarta, farther up the coast, grew rapidly to become Acapulco's rival in the popularity stakes. The stretch down to Manzanillo, labelled the Costa de Oro (Gold Coast), is attracting a number of

Wooded hills meet curving Mismaloya Beach in Puerto Vallarta, Jalisco

new resort hotels. Farther north and into the Gulf of California are older established resorts such as Mazatlán, Guaymas, and Bahía Kino, which have drawn North American visitors for decades with their fine fishing and sailing.

The development of tourism was given a boost in the 1970s, when the government set up a trust fund known as FONATUR. With careful selection and properly planned development, tourist centers like Ixtapa sprang up; its long beaches and strong surf contrast with the sheltered bay and more rustic

Above: gentle waves lap at Zihuatanejo
Left: sea foam scallops the sandy beach at Ixtapa

charms of neighboring Zihuatanejo. The latest FONATUR project is the development of the Bahías de Huatulco, an extensive area of nine bays along Oaxaca's southern coastline.

Such a vast area, with endless untouched jungle and beaches, is perhaps best appreciated from the window of an airplane. From this vantage point one can take in something of the contrasting land and seascapes. Golden sands with year-round swimming in transparent seas, set against a hinterland that is exotic, mysterious, and sometimes awe-inspiring, beckon the visitor to feast on the many delights of Mexico's west coast – still pristine over much of its length, and with the luxury of space not easily found in other resort destinations. (See map on pages 50–1.)

Acapulco

*F*or many years the "Pearl of the Pacific" reigned supreme as Mexico's number one resort. Now, as new areas have opened up, Acapulco's glamorous image as a playground for the jetset has faded somewhat. Nevertheless, Acapulco still has the name. And this, coupled with its spectacular setting, assures its continuing place in the top league of popular tourist resorts.

Whatever your taste, Acapulco offers an excellent climate and lively atmosphere, day and night, in a stunning setting. The first sight of Acapulco Bay from the coastal road above it wins over most people. With its gorgeous sweep of palm-fringed beach, high-rise hotels and backdrop of mountains, it is indeed spectacular. At night it becomes unforgettable, with hundreds of twinkling lights curving around the bay.

In its earlier days, Acapulco's western beaches and rocky coves drew the resort crowds. But popular beaches like Caleta and Caletilla were left to the locals as glitzy new hotels sprang up farther along the bay. These days, the tourist interest has shifted to Condesa and Los Hornos beaches, near the city's top-rated hotels. There is always a lively beach scene, with a wide range of aquatic activities, including parasailing, water-skiing, and sailing.

The Acapulco lifestyle is seductive. Pollution problems in the bay discourage many people from swimming in the sea, so visitors tend to spend the day sipping large cold drinks from the comfort of their poolside lounge chairs. The water is deliciously warm and pools are attractively designed, usually set in tropical gardens right by the sea.

It is worth getting away from your hotel's watery idyll to take in a few experiences, however. No visitor to Acapulco will want to miss the famous cliff divers of La Quebrada (see pages 80–1), whose midday and evening performances are positively breathtaking, or the Flying Men of Papantla who perform at the Acapulco Center. On a glass-bottom boat trip to Isla Roqueta, you can see beautiful multi-colored fish and marine plants, as well as an image of the Virgin of Guadalupe submerged 7m deep in the crystal-clear sea. Day or evening *fiesta* yacht cruises around the fine harbor have live music and dancing, and give an overall view of the city that is unmatched from the land.

Night time here is spectacular. The tropical air exudes an infectious excitement and, as the lights come on, the effect is magical. The classic way to greet the evening is to watch one of Acapulco's technicolor sunsets. The best place to view the setting sun is Pie de la Cuesta, a few kilometers north of town. Here, where the mountains meet the coastal plain of Coyuca Lagoon, you can stretch out in a hammock, gaze at the enormous waves crashing heavily on the long beach, and contemplate a vividly hued sunset that seems to envelop the whole sky.

Afterwards, the social round usually begins at the hotel bars, before people drift off for dinner. The place is teeming with eating places of every type, from elegant hotel restaurants with icy air-conditioning to open-air establishments in the hills offering glittering views of the bay. For many, the proper ending to the

The shimmering blue sea of Acapulco Bay is the perfect foil for dazzling white hotels

day is to dance the night away at one of the numerous deafening discos, which are an essential, if expensive, part of fashionable Acapulco.

Centro International Para Convivencia Infantil (CICI)

Large theme park for children, with water slides, pools, and dolphin shows. *Costera Miguel Alemán by Playa Icasos. Open: daily 10am–6pm. Admission charge.*

Fuerte De San Diego (Fort St. James)

A museum containing exhibits dating back to the founding of Acapulco is housed inside this fort, which was built between 1615 and 1617 to defend the port against marauding pirates. *Calle Morelos and Playa Hornitos. Tel: 82–38–28. Open: Tuesday to Sunday 10:30am–5pm. Admission charge.*

Papagayo Park

Many attractions for children, including an aviary, go-cart racing, roller-skating, boating on a small man-made lake. *Across from Playa Hornitos. Tel: 85–96–23. Open: daily 10am–8pm. Free.*

407km south of Mexico City. Information office: Costera Miguel Alemán 187. Tel: 86–91–71. Frequent flights from Mexico City (45 minutes), other Mexican and U.S. destinations. Regular bus services from Mexico City (about 7 hours).

HIGH FLIERS

Acapulco offers two very different types of spectacles, each involving daring feats that could justly be described as death-defying.

The story of Acapulco's celebrated cliff divers goes back to the early 1930s, when young boys would dive off the cliffs of La Quebrada for mere sport. With the arrival of tourism, the free show caught on, and today it is one of Acapulco's main attractions, rarely missed by any visitor. Athletic young men, perched on a sheer cliff over 40m above the sea, make a daring swallow dive into the narrow cove, calculating their timing to the split-second so as to enter the water on the up swell. By day the performances inspire admiration; by night they can literally take your breath away. Tension builds as the diver clambers up the rock face, prays before the chapel on top, and stands ready. At his given signal, flares are lit and down he goes! Everyone holds their breath until he reappears, seconds later, to loud acclaim. Spectators can view performances from the El Mirador Hotel and various public areas.

High diving into water is one thing, on to dry land quite another – especially as performed by the Flying Men of Papantla. Several evenings a week at the Acapulco Center this ancient Totonac ritual – believed to relate to the rain gods and the vanilla harvest – is re-enacted in all its drama and genuine danger. Five Indian men in colorful attire climb up a 100-foot-high pole to stand on a tiny platform. Once ready, four of them suddenly cast off into space and spiral downwards around the pole, twirling on the end of ropes attached to their feet, in 13 rotations. The fifth man stays atop the platform, playing a flute and beating a drum.

The participants are carefully selected young men, natives of Papantla, Veracruz, where the ritual originated. The dance is still performed in its native town, but for some years has been presented in various locales as a tourist attraction.

Cliff diving in Acapulco (left); Totonac Indians in El Tajín, "flying" and dancing

Huatulco beach, shaded by thatched palapas, invites a carefree stroll in the sand

BAHÍAS DE HUATULCO

Huatulco is the newest project of FONATUR, the Mexican government's National Trust Fund for tourism development. Located on Mexico's southern Pacific coast, the area marked for development covers nine bays and a tropical hinterland backed by the Sierra Madre. Following the same pattern as other big tourist developments, an isolated area of jungle and beaches was selected, with few inhabitants. Some 15 years after its initial planning, the resort is fast developing, with an airport, an increasing number of hotels, and a new town with a small marina.

Centered on Tangolunda Bay are several top-class hotels on the beachfront, with swimming pools and lush tropical landscaping. About 10 minutes away is the new inland town of La Crucesita, built in typical Mexican style with a main square and a bandstand. Boats depart from the marina at Santa Cruz (and several beachside hotels) for trips to other bays, some of which offer good swimming and snorkeling.

291km south of Oaxaca. Information office: Paseo B Juárez s/n, Tangolunda Bay. Tel: 7-01-77. Flights from Mexico City, Oaxaca and other domestic destinations. Buses from Oaxaca and Acapulco.

IXTAPA-ZIHUATANEJO

Although totally separate, the two resorts are served by the same airport and tend to be listed together. Yet another product of FONATUR's computer planning, Ixtapa has now grown into a fully fledged modern resort, complementing the fishing-village character of neighboring Zihuatanejo.

Ixtapa

Until the early 1970s, Ixtapa was an

isolated bay surrounded by dense virgin jungle. It has now developed into a sizeable resort with a string of modern hotels along a wide sandy beach much favored by Mexican families. Hotels offer a good selection of restaurants, and there are plenty of discos. All the popular sports can be practiced here: water-skiing, scuba diving, snorkeling, windsurfing, parasailing, and fishing. Good golfing is to be had at the two golf courses, and there is tennis and horseback riding.

Zihuatanejo

About 7km away, the old fishing village of Zihuatanejo lies in a lovely large bay formed by the convergence of jungle and mountains. Although it has seen some changes in recent years, its rustic charm, fun restaurants, and off-beat ambience provide a pleasing contrast to its modern neighbor. The sheltered bay provides good swimming from several beaches. Small hotels built amidst the foliage lead down to Playa la Ropa, one of the most popular beaches. A very enjoyable boat trip crosses the bay to the beach of Playa las Gatas. The clear, calm waters in this protected little cove offer wonderful snorkeling and diving. Open-air restaurants line the beach, which is popular with local families on weekends.
636km southwest of Mexico City.
Information offices: City Hall, Zihuatanejo.
Tel: 4–20–01. La Puerta Shopping Center,
Ixtapa. Te: 3–19–68. Regular flights from
Mexico City and other Mexican and US
destinations. Bus service from Mexico City.

Fishing boats rest between outings on Zihuatanejo's Municipal Beach

Manzanillo and the Costa de Oro

MANZANILLO

With its ample bay, Manzanillo has long been an important seaport. As far back as the 12th century, local Indians are thought to have had contact with Chinese traders, and it was from here that the Spanish conquerors set off for the Philippines and other lands. Hernán Cortés favored it enough to spend part of his retirement here. Nowadays it is a major shipping port, with a rail link running inland. Fishermen know it as a great shellfish center. For the visitor, however, the main focus of interest is the surrounding area.

It was the construction of Las Hadas (The Fairies) – a recreation center resembling a Moorish fantasy, dreamed up by a Bolivian tin magnate – that put Manzanillo on the map as a haven for the jetset. Internationally famous (and known as the exotic location of the film *10*), this spectacular Arabian Nights-style complex of dazzling white houses, turrets, and brilliantly colored tropical flowers lies on the southern slopes of the Santiago Peninsula, where other fine hotels are also located.

The surrounding hills are covered by ornate homes and villas, and development continues at a rapid pace, with the lights of Manzanillo town twinkling across the bay.

349km from Guadalajara. Information office: Boulevard Costera Miguel de la Madrid Km 9.5. Tel: 3–22–77. Direct flights from Mexico City and other Mexican destinations. Bus from Puerto Vallarta (5 hours).

Small fishing vessels lie at anchor in the historic harbor of Manzanillo

Living in a fantasy at Las Hadas, where even the lizards can take it easy

COSTA DE ORO

From Manzanillo north to Puerto Vallarta lies 286km of long sandy beaches and rocky coves backed by verdant jungle. As with other coastlines, it has acquired a name: the Costa de Oro (Gold Coast). Highway 200 veers inland here, with turn-offs to hotels and resorts, which are more easily reached by bus transfers from the airports of Manzanillo or Puerto Vallarta.

Barra de Navidad
The sleepy character of this small fishing village has been awakened by the nearby Pueblo Nuevo tourist complex, and the Isla Navidad developement, featuring new hotels, a marina, and golf course.
56km north of Manzanillo.

Costa de Careyes (Turtle Coast)
White beaches, palms trees, and azure lagoons, backed by tropical vegetation make up this region. The picturesque Bel-Air Costa Carreyes resort is an attractive feature of this beautiful stretch of coastline.
20km north of Tenacatita.

Melaque
Melaque's several small sandy beaches are surrounded by hills. An old-time favorite with Mexicans and Americans, the resort has plenty of moderately priced accommodations, bars, and restaurants.
11km north of Barra de Navidad.

Tenacatita
This is the location of a self-contained resort hotel with the delightful name of the Blue Bay Village Los Angeles Locos (The Crazy Angels), built around Tenacatita Bay. Visitors enjoy it for its good swimming, fishing, and air of tranquility.
19km north of Melaque.

The peace and quiet at Puerto Ángel seem heaven-sent to harried vacationers

MAZATLÁN

Mazatlán lies across from the southern tip of Baja California; an attractive resort encircled by cliffs, islands, and good beaches, with two large bays divided by prominent rocks. Less commercialized and away from the better known tourist circuit, it has always had a special appeal for Americans and Mexicans.

Mazatlán is a big sport-fishing center (marlin and sailfish tournaments are held here), and all necessary equipment can be rented. There are facilities for all the popular water sports, such as sailing, parasailing, water-skiing, and scuba diving. Swimmers must take care, as the waves can be very rough in certain parts. Surfers head for the Playa Las Olas (Beach of High Waves) and some of the beaches north of town. For landlubbers, there's golf and tennis.

A special feature of Mazatlán is its long *malecón* (coastal promenade), where you can take a stroll by the Pacific – very atmospheric at sunset or at night by the light of a full moon. Along the *malecón* is a towering rock known as El Mirador (The Lookout), from which local boys make daring daytime dives into a crevice,

a sort of mini version of the famous Acapulco cliff divers.

The center of town is lively, with many bars and restaurants frequented by the younger set. A fun way of exploring is with the *pulmonías*, a specialty of Mazatlán. These curious open-air three-wheel taxis, resembling a motor scooter, puff their way up steep hills (their name means "lungs"). The town is all ups and downs, offering several panoramic hilltop views over the bays.

Although short on historical sights, Mazatlán has a few places of special interest.

Acuario Mazatlán

This modern, hexagonal aquarium features an immense shark tank and smaller tanks with over 250 species of marine life, as well as a museum of marine life and a botanical garden.
111 Avenida de los Deportes, near Avenida del Mar. Tel: 81–78–15. Open: daily 9:30am–6:30pm. Admission charge.

505km northwest of Guadalajara.
Information office: Avenida Camarón Sábalo.
Tel: 16–51–60/5. Flights from Mexico City,

other Mexican and U.S. destinations. Buses from Tijuana and Mexico City.

PUERTO ÁNGEL

This old fishing village, once a prominent seaport; is tucked away in a small turquoise bay on Oaxaca's southern coast. Time has largely passed it by, and the place is strictly a spot for low-budget travelers looking for an outdoor life in casual surroundings. Most visitors head for the nearby beaches of Panteón or Zipolite, a particular favorite. Located 6km west of town, it offers good swimming, surfing and a carefree existence lounging about in a hammock.
83km southeast of Puerto Escondido on Road 200. Daily bus from Oaxaca.

PUERTO ESCONDIDO

Northwest of Puerto Ángel is Puerto Escondido (Hidden Port), which lies in a bay flanked by hills covered with exotic vegetation. Although more developed than Puerto Ángel, it still retains a rustic charm and offers total relaxation. The village center has now been closed to traffic and turned into a shopping and tourist area. Along the beach are cafés and restaurants. Away from the center, other good beaches include the popular Puerto Angelito, a rocky little cove with hammocks and a restaurant.

Surfing is a big attraction in and around Puerto Escondido. To the east is Zicatela beach, renowned for its gigantic waves and strong undertow. Top-class surfing champions come here for competitions.
264km south of Oaxaca. Flights from Mexico City. Buses from Oaxaca.

Some work, some play in Puerto Escondido; the catch is in and the surf is up!

Puerto Vallarta

Situated in the center of the wide Bahía de (Bay of) Banderas, Puerto Vallarta is surrounded by cliffs and mountains covered by dense jungle. Until the early 1960s, it was a remote fishing village that rarely even appeared on road maps. Then *Night of the Iguana* was filmed on nearby Punta Mismaloya, and its star, Richard Burton, attended by his paramour Elizabeth Taylor, was the focus of international interest. When they bought property in the hills, the village began to acquire a certain mystique. Today, with its superb beaches, it is one of Mexico's most popular resorts, whose casual ambience appeals to a younger, more Bohemian type of clientele than does Acapulco.

The old town still retains much of its original Mexican flavor, with narrow cobbled streets leading up into the hills. This downtown area is a focal point, bustling with shops, bars and tourists. Strung along the coast towards the airport are most of the resort's top deluxe hotels, where fine beaches and tempting pools in tropical gardens provide good swimming. The Cuale River, which runs through the town, divides to form the small Isla del Río Cuale. Here are shops and restaurants, and an exotic view of the river against the backdrop of lush green mountains.

The Marina Vallarta offers luxury accommodations, golf and tennis, a commercial center, and slips for some 300 boats. Fishermen still go out in the small hours to provide one of the staple foods for local families. A favorite beach is the Playa de los Muertos, which is always charged with activity. There is excellent swimming and every variety of water sport, from parasailing and water-skiing to sailing and deep-sea fishing. Donkey polo and horse riding along the shore are also popular pastimes. Thatched-roof restaurants and bars add to the scene, which is relaxed, informal, and inviting.

Puerto Vallarta is known for its lively nightlife with no shortage of discos. People usually start off with a drink to watch the sunset (they can be magnificent here) and continue with dinner and maybe some dancing. Many of the hotel lobby bars have a terrific atmosphere, enhanced by tropical music. One of the most popular excursions out of Puerto Vallarta is the boat trip to the wild jungle beach of Yelapa, across

The streets and homes of old Puerto Vallarta gracefully yield to age and the elements

Hills overlook the tidy beach of Playa Mismaloya in Puerto Vallarta

Banderas Bay (see pages 90–1). Other boat trips take you to the beaches at Las Ánimas, Piedra Blanca, and Mismaloya. Regular excursions explore the jungle hinterland, by coach, jeep, or on horseback.

Some 12km north of town is Nuevo Vallarta, a resort built on a landscape of attractive estuaries and intricate canals. It offers luxurious hotels, a shopping center, and a large marina. The road continues to the small resort of Bucerías; then follows the curve of the bay to some lovely isolated beaches including those of Cruz de Huanacaxtla, Arena Blanca, and Destiladeras.

327km west of Guadalajara. Information office: City Hall, Avenida Juárez. Tel: 2–02–42. Flights from Mexico City and other domestic destinations. International flights from U.S. destinations.

Puerto Vallarta to Yelapa

This is a popular excursion across the Bahía de Banderas to the jungle beach of Yelapa, with a short hike through the vegetation to a waterfall. *Allow a full day.*

Go to the Terminal Marítima (Marina) at about 8:30am and make your selection. The largest boat is the Sarape. *One beer is included in the price, but no lunch. The boat sets off at about 9am.*

1 PUERTO VALLARTA'S COASTLINE
The *Sarape* has three decks, with good viewing from the top

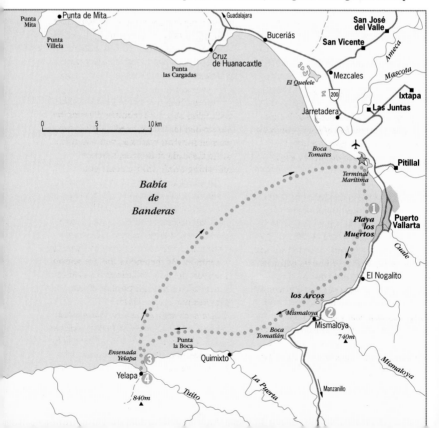

deck. The first part of the journey takes you slowly along the resort's long shoreline, with hotels standing out against the densely wooded mountains. After a while you will see the church tower, with its open-work crown, rising above the village.

Gradually the hotels and condominiums thin out and the terrain becomes more rugged. About one and a half hours later, you will pass by Mismaloya Beach and Los Arcos.

2 MISMALOYA

The beach still lives on its reputation as the setting for the film *Night of the Iguana* (you will doubtless be reminded of it). Beachside food and drink stands are plentiful, and the warm waters and exotic marine plants invite exploration on another occasion. In front, several giant boulders rise from the sea to form natural arches – hence their name, Los Arcos. They are home to a bird colony and a popular area for snorkeling.

The boat continues along tropical coastlines until you spy the distant beach of Yelapa, tucked away at the foot of jungle-covered mountains. A small boat then takes passengers in shifts to the nearby jetty.

3 YELAPA

The setting here is magnificent, with a backdrop of tropical mountains towering around you. The beach is littered with open-air restaurants and vendors. In the bay is plenty of activity, with swimming, water-skiing, and speed boats whizzing around. You can settle down to an informal lunch on arrival, or proceed with the waterfall excursion.

Eager boatmen offer you rides from the beach. Determine the price before accepting. After scrambling aboard, you are off on a 5-minute or so ride across to the tiny Indian village of Yelapa.

Catching a sea breeze on a touring catamaran

4 THROUGH THE JUNGLE

After a somewhat undignified exit from the boat, you arrive in tiny Yelapa village; curious children, stray dogs, and washing lines make an unexpected contrast to TV satellite dishes. Someone will lead the route, which goes up some rough steps and over large boulders as you enter the jungle proper, amidst palms and lush tropical vegetation. The walk takes about 20 minutes. Passing by a river bed far below, used by the local women for their washing, you will come to La Cascada el Bosque, where a refreshing drink will welcome you.

Just beyond is the waterfall. In a dramatic setting, with huge boulders amidst the encroaching jungle, a waterfall cascades over steep rocks to a pool which, during and after the rainy season, is quite full and tempting enough to swim in. By the end of the dry season, however, the waterfall can be reduced to a mere trickle and the pool turns an unappealing copper color.

Return to the edge of the bay, where a boat will soon arrive to take you back to Yelapa Beach. At about 2pm, a signal horn will be heard from the Sarape *for departure at 2:50pm, arriving in Puerto Vallarta at 5pm.*

Southeastern Mexico and the Yucatán

*T*his giant land mass, which completes Mexico's horn shape, encompasses the states of Chiapas, Tabasco, Campeche, Yucatán, and Quintana Roo. It is bounded on the north by the Gulf of Mexico and on the south by the Pacific. To the east is the Caribbean, while to the southeast Mexico shares a border with Guatemala and Belize.

The range of attractions within this region is enormous, from ancient ruins, Indian villages, and colonial towns to modern beach resorts, with a striking diversity of landscapes.

In Chiapas, steamy jungles contrast cloud-covered mountains, where temperatures can be cool. The state offers some stunning scenery, with lakes, waterfalls, rivers, and a dramatic canyon, in addition to a wealth of flora and fauna and a fascinating look at the life of

SOUTHEASTERN MEXICO AND THE YUCATAN

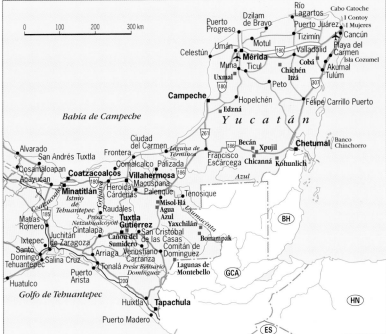

indigenous peoples. Campeche is characterized by rolling hills and tropical rain forests, while the Yucatán is a flat limestone shelf covered by low scrubland, with underground rivers, caves, and *cenotes*, or natural sinkholes. The Yucatecans are known for their smiling faces and friendliness. Their small villages with oval thatched-roof huts are a delight to visit. Quintana Roo is largely a wilderness of jungle, swamps, and lakes. However, the development of popular Cancún and other beach resorts

down its eastern Caribbean coast has put it firmly on the map. Perhaps the biggest attraction, however, is the treasure of archaeological sites scattered throughout the area. This region was the home of the Maya, whose magnificent cities bear testimony to a great past. The major ruins are easily reached: Palenque, set deep in the jungle; Chichén Itzá, the most famous and best-restored of the Yucatán's Mayan ruins; and magnificent Uxmal, one of the best examples of Classic Mayan architecture. Others are less accessible, but all make an important contribution to the fascination of southeastern Mexico.

Palenque's Temples of the Cross, the Foliated Cross and the Sun (left to right)

Cancún

*I*n a very real sense, Cancún is the child of a silicon chip! The Mexican government used a computer to select an ideal location for a new resort, and it came up with Cancún, a strip of virgin sand and deserted jungle on the coast of Quintana Roo. This was the first project of FONATUR, a government agency set up in the 1970s to develop new tourist resorts with a proper infrastructure. Included in the concept was also the provision of local employment and a boost to the region's economy.

Cancún has proved a success story. Since construction got underway in 1974, it has grown into Mexico's most popular resorts, thanks to powdery white beaches, clear turquoise waters, and all-encompassing facilities. Its proximity to Florida makes it a convenient spot for travelers from Europe and the East Coast of the United States.

Another point in Cancún's favor is its pleasant year-round climate, as cool sea breezes prevent it from getting overly hot during the summer months. Do be aware, however, that in autumn this coastline can be subject to strong winds

Red skin, white sand, blue sea: avoid only the first while relaxing on Cancún's beach

and unsettled weather, including the occassional hurricane.

The resort is divided into two areas. Downtown Cancún is made up of shopping malls in modernistic styles with stores and boutiques, restaurants, and discos. There are also handicraft centers, but prices are often higher here than elsewhere in Mexico, because everything is brought in from outside.

Quite separate to the town is the Zona Hotelera (Hotel Zone), which extends along 19km of sandbar, with the Caribbean on one side and a lagoon on the other. This thin strip of land is connected it to the mainland by bridges. Hotels are plentiful and come in an assortment of categories and shapes (architects have had a field day here). The sand is soft white powder, remaining cool to walk on, and the turquoise shades of the Caribbean are unbeatable, offering

Underwater diving at Chankanab, Cozumel Island

idyllic conditions for swimming in certain parts. The best and safest beaches are those on the Bay of Isla Mujeres. Around the eastern end of the peninsula, a strong undertow and heavy surf can make swimming very dangerous. Always look for the red flag warnings on beaches.

A wide variety of aquatic sports can be enjoyed here: windsurfing, jet-skiing, and parasailing are very popular. Motor and sail boats, Hobie cats, canoes, and kayaks are all available to rent. There is sailing, deep-sea fishing, and diving and snorkeling; good areas are around the reefs between Cancún and Isla Mujeres. Equipment can be rented from the major hotels or marinas. There is also golf at the 18-hole Pok-Ta-Pok Robert Trent Course and tennis at the courts adjoining some hotels. Many evenings offer spectacular sunsets, while at night the pace is fast and furious, with an abundance of discos and night-spots and drinking

establishments to choose from.

Numerous one-day excursions can be made. There are daily trips to the islands of Isla Mujeres and Cozumel (see page 97), cruises on the Nichupte Lagoon for snorkeling, and night cruises. Glass-bottomed boats are ideal for viewing the rich underwater marine life, while a visit to the bird sanctuary on Isla Contoy (see page 140) is another option. But don't miss a trip down the so-called Cancún–Tulum corridor to the Mayan ruins at Tulum (see page 109), with stop-offs at some of the beautiful lagoons and bays on the way, including the Sian Ka'an Biosphere Reserve (see pages 140–1).

321km east of Mérida, on the northeastern tip of the Yucatán Peninsula. Information office: Avenida Tulum 26. Tel: 84-80-73. Regular flights from Mexico City and other domestic destinations, Miami, other U.S. and European destinations. Also charters from the U.S. and Europe. Buses from Mérida.

CANCÚN–TULUM CORRIDOR

This coastal stretch, also known as the Costa Turquesa (Turquoise Coast) runs for 160km south of Cancún. A well-kept two-lane motorway (slowly being widened to four lanes) runs inland through scrub forests, with an increasing number of short turn-offs to beach resorts, lagoons, a marina developement, theme park, and a variety of attractions. Driving south from Cancún, look out for the following towns.

Akumal

Akumal lies in an idyllic Caribbean setting: small bungalows dotting a palm-fringed beach, soft white sand curving around a sparkling bay. This is a well-known center for snorkeling and skin-diving, offering expert instruction and ideal safe conditions.
101km south of Cancún.

Playa del Carmen

This has grown into a popular resort among the younger set, with plenty of action along its long sandy beach, which is lined with hotels, bars, and restaurants. Ferries operate from here to the tranquil island of Cozumel.
66km south of Cancún.

Puerto Aventuras

The ambitious development of Puerto Aventuras, farther down the coast, caters to the affluent. It is attractively designed, with hotels, villas and condominiums, shopping centers, restaurants, and an 18-hole golf course. A major feature is the deep-water marina, which can accommodate large luxury yachts.
97km south of Cancún.

Share Xel-Há's lagoon with colorful fish

Tulum

See page 109.

119km south of Cancún.

Xcaret

Now developed into a large "Eco-Archaelogical Park," Xcaret's attractions include an underground swim through subterranean caves, cavorting with dolphins, snorkeling, a tropical aquarium and butterfly pavilion, and spectacular evening shows. Small Maya ruins are dotted about the place.

71km south of Cancún. Between Playa del Carmen and Akumal. Open: Monday to Saturday 8.30am–8.30pm, Sunday 8.30am–5.30pm. Admission charge

Xel-Há

Aptly described as a "natural aquarium," the Xel-Há national park consists of four interlocking lagoons in stunning shades of turquoise and blue. Swimming and snorkeling are permitted in its crystal clear waters which abound with tropical fish. Equipment is available for rent.

122km south of Cancún. Between Akumal and Tulum. Open: daily 8am–5pm. Admission charge.

CARIBBEAN ISLANDS

Cozumel

Cozumel (Island of Swallows in Mayan), 53km long and 17km wide, is the larger of the two islands that lie off the northeast coast of the Yucatán Peninsula. With beautiful white sandy beaches, palm trees, and turquoise waters, it offers all the relaxation of a desert-island hideaway. The principal town, San Miguel, has a lively square with restaurants, bars, and shops.

The reefs around the island are a paradise for snorkeling and scuba diving.

The most famous is the Palancar Reef, about a mile offshore. Others include the reefs of San Francisco, Maracaíbo, Colombia, Santa Rosa Wall, and Yaceb. Chancanab Lagoon, on the west coast of the island, also offers excellent swimming and snorkeling amidst tropical fish.

20km from the mainland. There are ferries from Playa del Carmen, about 1 hour 15 minutes. It also connects by air with Mexico City and U.S. destinations.

The coral reef is close to shore at El Garrafón National Park, on Isla Mujeres

Isla Mujeres

The tiny island of Isla Mujeres (Island of Women) lies north of Cozumel. It measures only 8km by 1km and can easily be explored on foot or by rented moped. The scene is relaxed and informal, with a special appeal for the young and adventurous. There is magnificent snorkeling and scuba diving at the well-known El Garrafón National Park, a coral reef just offshore with shoals of tropical fish. Los Manchones, on the southern end of the island, is another good spot.

10km from the Yucatán mainland. There are regular ferries from Puerto Juárez and Punta Sam, which also carry cars.

Chichén Itzá

*T*he old Mayan/Toltec city of Chichén Itzá is one of Mexico's great archaeological sites, and a highlight for any visitor to the Yucatán. The site extends over a large clearing in the jungle, and is considered one of the best-preserved pre-Columbian sites in the country.

Chichén means "place of the well" in Mayan. The Itzá were a Mayan sect who occupied the original settlement, which dates back as early as AD 360. Although the city later fell into decline, it flourished again under the Toltecs, who arrived in the 10th century and built on to many of the existing buildings. It reached its peak in the 11th and 12th centuries, but was soon abandoned.

The site is divided into the northern and southern groups. Start with the northern group (or "new Chichén"), which is dominated by the magnificent El Castillo (The Castle), or Pyramid of Kukulkán. Each side has a stairway of 91 steps, which, including the top platform,

---

THE DESCENT OF KUKULKÁN

The Mayas believed that their great sun god Kukulkán – also known as Quetzalcóatl, the plumed serpent – returned to earth at the spring and autumn equinoxes. This long-lost legend was rediscovered by an archaeologist who found that, on those days, the serrated shadow cast by the corner angle of El Castillo forms the body of a serpent gliding down the northwest stairway to the carved head of the bloodthirsty god. The equinoxes occur on or around March 21 and September 22, and each year vast crowds come from all over to witness this intriguing spectacle.

---

makes a total of 365. A heavy chain assists the climb to the top, which offers a magnificent view of the site. Down below, a small entrance leads up dark narrow slippery steps to two inner chambers, containing a red "Jaguar Throne" with jade eyes and a reclining *chacmool* figure. (check for opening times.)

The Templo de los Guerreros (Temple of the Warriors) is an impressive building of large columns and a *chacmool* altar. Below is the Grupo de las Mil Columnas (Group of a Thousand Columns), with carvings of plumed serpents. Other structures include the Tzompantli (Wall of Skulls), the Platform of the Eagles and Tigers, and the Temple of the Jaguars. The Juego de Pelota (Ball Court) is the largest of its kind, and has excellent acoustics.

A path into the jungle leads to the sinister Cenote de los Sacrificios (Sacred Well), where the skeletons of young girls were discovered along with treasures of jade, gold, and other artifacts.

Structures of major interest in the southern group ("old Chichén") include the newly reconstructed Tumba del Gran Sacerdote (Tomb of the High Priest); El Caracol (The Snail), an ancient observatory, with a spiral stairway leading to the top, where the Maya studied the solar system and made astronomical calculations; the Edificio de las Monjas

A reclining *chacmool* figure on the Temple of the Warriors gazes across the site

SITE PLAN
1 Juego de Pelota
2 Temazcalli
3 Juego de Pelota
4 Columnata del Noroeste
5 Templo de las Mesas
6 Tzompantli
7 Casa de las Aguilas
8 Templo de los Jaguares
9 Edifico Sur
10 Templo Norte
11 Casa de los Metates
12 Templo de Venado
13 Chichán-chob (Casa Colorada)
14 Iglesia
15 Templo de los Tableros
16 Akab-Dzib

CHICHÉN ITZÁ

(Nunnery); Chichán-chob or Casa Colorada (Red House) and the Iglesia (Church). Son et lumière shows take place every evening, except in bad weather. *120km east of Mérida. Open: daily 8am–5pm. Admission charge. Most visitors take a tour from Mérida.*

THE MAYAN WORLD

*"They flattened their heads and foreheads, their ears bored with rings in them.
Their faces were generally good, and not very brown, but without beards,
for they scorched them when young, that they might not grow.
Their hair was long like women, and in tresses, with which they made a garland
about the head, and a little tail hung behind."*

This was how the Spaniard Antonio de Herrera described what he saw in "the Indies," about a hundred years after Cortés first landed in Mexico. The people he wrote of were the Maya, whose culture flourished between AD 300 and 900. They built their huge, stately pyramids all over Central America, from Yucatán to Honduras, and achieved this feat without the use of the wheel, beasts of burden, or any metal in their constructions. At their peak, they perfected the most complex writing system in the hemisphere, mastered mathematics, and created an astronomical calendar of amazing accuracy.

Their society was a rigidly stratified one: priest-nobles and warriors at the top of the social pyramid, then a middle class of merchants, administrators, overseers, and artisans, and slaves at the lowest ranks. Their gods and sub-gods were many and greedy, ruling people's existence with bloodthirsty harshness. Appeasing them meant human torture and sacrifice, usually virgins thrown into the sacred *cenotes* (wells) which are the Yucatán's only sources of fresh water.

Years of enthusiastic scholarship and painstaking excavation and analysis have produced a picture of what life might well have been like before the Conquest:

A typical family of perhaps five to seven members arose before dawn to a breakfast of hot chocolate or, if they were poor, a thick maize drink, plus *tamales* or the flat maize pancakes called *tortillas*. Their one-room thatched house was made of poles woven together, and covered with dried mud. Meals of corn, squash, beans, and the occasional rabbit or turkey were prepared by the women, who also wove, while the men worked in the fields or built temples and pyramids.

At the end of the day, the family would chant and pray and perform a ritual bloodletting, which was their central act of piety. High points in the year centered on attending royal marriages, ceremonies

Myths and rituals are portrayed through art at Xochicalco (carving) and Cacaxtla (murals)

thought, painted themselves black until marriage, and later engaged in ritual scarring and tattooing.

Although their culture disappeared centuries ago, the Maya did not. It's estimated that 1.2 million Maya live in the state of Chiapas, and nearly 5 million more are spread throughout the Yucatán, Belize, Guatamala, Honduras, and El Salvador. These once-proud people are now usually to be found, impoverished, among the forgotten of their country. The "Mundo

related to the calendar, or the elaborate sacrifice of a captive or a loser of the ball game. They beautified themselves by filing their teeth and inlaying them with round chips of jade or pyrite. The sloping foreheads and flattened heads they so admired were achieved by strapping boards round the heads of their infants; parents encouraged the much-prized crossed eyes by hanging small beads over the noses of their children. Young men, it is

Maya Project" is trying to promote awareness of their culture, past and present, and encourage a tourism that respects both the people and the environment.

Panama hats by the stack in Mérida

MÉRIDA

Mérida is the capital of the Yucatán, and the main base for visiting Uxmal (see pages 110–11) and Chichén Itzá (see pages 98–9). Industrial growth has changed its sleepy image of old, but the place still has elegant mansions and the graceful traditions of its people. It was founded in 1542 on the ruins of a much older Indian city, and its great wealth derived from *henequen* (a fiber product used to make rope). Today, local people are renowned for fine leatherwork, Panama hats, and embroidered shirts.

Two of Mérida's most attractive features are its delightful zócalo and bustling daily market.

Casa de Montejo

Now occupied by Banamex, the handsome 16th-century Montejo House is noted for its finely decorated plateresque façade.
Calle 63, Plaza Principal. Open: weekdays 9am–5pm.

Catedral

This 16th-century cathedral, with a fortress-like exterior and a fairly plain interior, is the largest on the Yucatán peninsula.
Plaza Principal. Open: Monday to Saturday 6am–noon, 4–8pm, Sunday 6am–1pm, 4–8pm.

Palacio Cantón

This houses the Museo Regional de Antropología and gives an insight into the Yucatán's history.
Calle 43, at Paseo de Montejo. Tel: 23-05-57. Open: Tuesday to Saturday 9am–6pm, Sunday 9am–2pm. Admission charge (Sunday free).

Palacio del Gobierno

The elegant, late 19th-century Governor's Palace encloses a pretty patio, and the staircase walls are covered with symbolic and mythical murals.
Plaza Principal.

Palacio Municipal

The Town Hall, built in 1735, features arches and a clock tower.
Opposite the Catedral.

1,497km northeast of Mexico City. Information office: Teatro Peon Contreras, Calle 59. Tel: 24-92-90. Flights from the U.S., Mexico City, and domestic destinations.

OTHER SIGHTS
Bonampak

These Mayan ruins deep in the jungle of eastern Chiapas are not easy to reach. Bonampak (Painted Walls in Mayan) is famous for its frescos depicting pre-battle rituals, warriors, and battle scenes.
130km southeast of Palenque. Open: daily 8am–4pm. Charter planes from Palenque, Tuxtla Gutiérrez, San Cristóbal de las Casas, or Comitán, or by road in dry season.

Cañon del Sumidero

Boat trips along the Grijalva River pass beside the sheer walls of this stratified canyon, giving a close-up view of the wildlife (see page 135). You can also look down into the canyon from several *miradores* (viewpoints) on the road above. *Chiapa de Corzo is 15km east of Tuxtla.*

Cascadas Agua Azul

These jungle waterfalls present a dazzling sight of waterfalls in beautiful shades of turquoise tumbling over limestone rocks.

Some 42km northeast, a left turn off the road to Palenque leads to the delightful waterfall of Misol-Há, which thunders down into a pool. A wonderful spot for swimming in lush surroundings. *55km south of Palenque village. Admission charge. Best by own vehicle or by an organized excursion from Palenque.*

Lagunas de Montebello

These lakes are renowned for their different hues of blue, green, and violet, and are surrounded by mountains, quiet pine forests, and wildlife (see page 135). *103km southeast of San Cristóbal de las Casas. Free. Buses from San Cristóbal via Comitán.*

Rio Bec Group

An archaeological zone of several sites. Most accessible are Chicanná, Becán, and Xpujil, with guide services recommended for visiting Calakmul, Balankú, Rio Bec itself, and others in the area. Off Highway 186 to Chetumal are the ruins of Kohunlich in their exotic surroundings. *Main zone: 120km west of Chetumal. Admission charge for some sites. Use own vehicle or organised tour.*

Yaxchilán

Set high on a loop of the Usumacinta River, in jungle inhabited by Lacandon Indians (see page 133), these Mayan ruins were built between AD 500 and 800. *32km east of Bonampak. Open: daily 8am–4pm. Admission charge.*

Sumidero Canyon and the Grijalva River

Palenque

Some consider these Mayan ruins – once highly colored – to be the most spectacular in Mexico, and a visit is highly recommended. Lying in the humid tropical growth of Chiapas, they seem steeped in brooding mystery, reminiscent of the lost cities of bygone times. Palenque was occupied from about 300 BC to the end of the 8th century, when it was abandoned and slowly devoured by vegetation.

At the entrance are little stalls set up by local Lacandon Indians, recognizable by their long straight black hair and proud demeanor. Entering the site, you will pass two small ruined temples on the right before coming upon the most interesting building of all. The Templo de las Inscripciones (Temple of the Inscriptions) dates from the end of the 7th century. In 1949, down in the bowels of the temple, archaeologist Alberto Ruiz Lhuillier uncovered a hidden crypt containing the sarcophagus of chieftain Pakal, surrounded by treasures. It was the first time in Mexico that a tomb was found inside a temple. Recent explorations have unearthed more such tombs in the region. An easy climb from the rear takes you to the top of the temple, which has magnificent carvings and glyphs of Mayan scenes. From here,

The deteriorated façade of the Temple of the Foliated Cross reveals architectural structure

you can descend to the crypt and view the royal tomb. Take care with the poor lighting and slippery stairway.

The grassy slopes of the site are scattered up and down with other buildings. Atop a large platform is the imposing Palacio (Palace), which was evidently occupied by dignitaries for special ceremonies. Delicate carvings also adorn these walls. Behind the palace, on the right, lies a curious little group of temples with roofcombs, reached by a short excursion through the jungle and across a small shallow stream. Known as the Templo del Sol (Temple of the Sun), Templo de la Cruz (Cross), and Templo de la Cruz Foliada (Foliated Cross), they are all perched high up on grassy mounds.

The oldest excavated building is the Templo del Conde (Temple of the Count). From the top of the adjacent Grupo Norte (Northern Group) is a good view of the site. Beyond this is a small museum with clay figurines, jewels of jade, shell, mother-of-pearl, and obsidian, and other artifacts. A nearby beauty spot overlooks a waterfall.

The dense tropical vegetation in and around the site is magnificent. If you want to explore the interior, go with a guide and keep to the paths. Linger awhile under the canopy of these tall jungle trees and listen to the birdsong or cries of the howler monkeys. The almost mystical harmony between these exotic surroundings and

PALENQUE

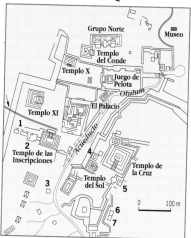

SITE PLAN
1 Templo XII
2 Templo XIII
3 Casa del Jaguar
4 Edifico XIV
5 Templo de la Cruz Foliada
6 Templo XVIII
7 Templo XVIIIa

Temple of the Cross (top); tomb lid (above) shows Pakal with snakes, monsters, and sun god

the ancient, human-made splendors makes this a very special place. (Use insect repellent freely.)

143km southeast of Villahermosa, near Palenque village. Information office: Avenida Juárez y Absolo. Tel: 5–07–60. Site – open: daily 8am–5pm; tomb – open: 10am–4pm. Admission charge (Sundays and holidays free). Most people take a day's excursion from Villahermosa. Otherwise, there are bus services from Villahermosa and other towns, and flights from other parts of southern Mexico.

THE CHAMULAS

The highlands around San Cristóbal de las Casas are inhabited by about 65,000 people descended from two Maya groups, the Tzotzils, and the Tzeltals. Although close geographically, each group speaks its own dialect, has its own traditions, and preserves its distinctive customs and traditions.

Among the most interesting are the Tzotzil-speaking Chamulas, who live in the district of San Juan Chamula, not far from San Cristóbal. The tiny village focuses around a small mystical church, which is the scene of strange spiritual practices with pre-Christian influences. The floor is strewn with pine needles and stuck with candles, which fill the church. Chamulas chant amidst clouds of incense while *curanderos* (healers) cure ailments, uttering incantations as they work with a rather unusual combination

surrounding villages. The Chamula men are usually in white, while a black tunic signifies some position of authority. The ruling elders, attired in special costumes, with ribboned hats and a staff, sit outside the church and help sort out the villagers' problems.

People and their handicrafts: Chamula Indians in the plaza at Chamula; examples of weaving and traditional garments in San Cristóbal

of ingredients, including a chicken, eggs, *posh* (the local firewater), Pepsi Cola, and a candle.

The Chamulas worship John the Baptist and some 40 other saints, whose statues are adorned with mirrors. Sometimes the statues are tied up and temporarily "put in jail" as a punishment for not responding to a solicitation! Visitors may enter the church after paying a nominal fee at the small office across the square. Note, however, that photography within the church is strictly forbidden.

The Sunday morning market, which takes place in front of the church, is the meeting place for Indians from all the

San Juan Chamula is also renowned for its numerous religious festivals, which combine pagan and Christian beliefs. These are organized by a selected major-domo, or senior person in charge, who must pay all costs, including food and drink. One of the liveliest festivals is Carnival, just before Lent, when the participants wear masks, take part in races, and run barefoot over live coals.

SAN CRISTÓBAL DE LAS CASAS

This curious little town, set high among the cloud forests, is Spanish in style, with cobbled streets, colored houses with tiled roofs, and some fine churches. The place, which is small and easy to explore, seems still to belong to the 18th century, but the environment is predominantly Indian. In recent years, however, the huge influx of Chamulas, expelled from their villages for converting to Protestantism (a result of U.S. missionaries at work), and increasing tourism are gradually changing the place.

Catedral

The main square, Plaza 31 de Marzo, is dominated by this large, early baroque building. Started in 1547, it was substantially transformed in the 18th century. Beyond the stark façade, the church contains gilded altars and two remarkable paintings: the *Virgin of Sorrows* to the left of the altar, and *The Magdalena* inside the sacristy.

Central Marketplace

Beside the Santo Domingo church, a splendid assortment of fruit, vegetables, medicinal herbs, flowers, and live poultry is sold daily by traders whose costumes denote their tribe (the ribbons on the Zinacantecos' hats indicate how many children they have). The liveliest market day is Saturday.

Na-Bolom (House of the Jaguar)

Founded by Danish archaeologist Frans Blom and his Swiss photographer wife Trudi, both deceased, who devoted years to studying and helping the Indians of

Church of Santo Domingo and its neighboring Chamula craft market in San Cristóbal

the region, this now runs as a study center (and guesthouse), with small museums, and an extensive library of books on the Maya.
Avenida Vicente Guerrero. Tel: 8–14–18. Open: Tuesday to Sunday 10am–1:30pm, 4:30–7pm. English-speaking tours at 4:30pm. Admission charge.

Templo de Santo Domingo
St. Dominic's Church is notable for its impressive baroque exterior, gilt rococo interior, and carved gilt pulpit. In front of the church, Chamula women have installed a mini market selling brightly colored woven goods.
Santo Domingo, on the corner of Lázaro Cárdenas and Nicaragua.

83km northeast of Tuxtla Gutiérrez. Information office: Palacio Municipal. Tel: 8–01–35. Regular buses from Tuxtla Gutiérrez (about 2 hours). Note: Early in 1994, San Cristóbal and other towns in the area were stormed by a group calling themselves the Zapatista National Liberation Army and demanding better conditions for the indigenous people. Since then the area has remained relatively calm, with occasional reports of localized skirmishes and outbreaks of hostilities.

SAN JUÁN CHAMULA
See pages 106–7.

TULUM
While it cannot compete with the greats in terms of architectural merit, Tulum does score points on location. As the only sizeable Mayan city found on the coast, its dramatic setting on a clifftop overlooking the Carribbean is an attraction in itself. The stone fortifications that surround it were a response to the constant wars stemming

Visit Tulum in the early morning, then retreat to the beach when tour buses arrive later

from the region's political instability. Tulum dates back to the 13th century. In 1518 it was sighted by a Spanish expedition, led by Juan de Grijalva, as it passed the coast. The Spaniards were impressed by Tulum's size and splendor, likening it to Seville. Part of the old surrounding wall remains today.

The prominent Castillo (Castle) commands a splendid view of the coral-dotted sea. Above the entrance is a stucco sculpture of a "descending god," one of several in Tulum. The Templo del Dios Descendente and the Templo de los Frescos also feature these sculptures above the main doorways of each building. The significance of the recurring figure is open to interpretation, including some theories about earthly visitations by aliens from other planets!

Another place of archaeological interest is Cobá, 44km to the northwest. This once great ceremonial center, never found by the Spaniards, flourished from the 5th century to the end of the 12th, and the ruins spread over a large area of humid jungle and lakes. It can only be reached by car or organized excursion.
Cobá – open: daily 8am–5pm. Admission charge (Sundays and holidays free).

119km south of Cancún. Can only be reached by car.

Uxmal

*T*he famous archaeological site of Uxmal is perhaps the most elegant of all Mexico's Mayan ruins. Along with Chichén Itzá, it represents one of the Yucatán's major attractions. Smaller and more compact than Chichén, it contains some of the most beautiful examples of classic Mayan architecture. Uxmal, which means "thrice built," was probably founded in the 6th century AD. It became an important ceremonial center and flourished between the 7th and 10th centuries. Its monuments, covered with delicate carvings, belong to the typical Puuc style of the Maya Classic period.

As Chichén Itzá developed, Uxmal's importance gradually waned until the latter lapsed into obscurity. Soaring above you as you enter the site is the imposing Pirámide del Adivino (Pyramid of the Soothsayer). According to a curious legend, it was built in one night by a dwarf with the help of his mother, a witch. Four stairways lead steeply up the pyramid. With the help of a rope you can climb up two of the stairways to the temple at the top, which offers a magnificent view of the site and surrounding jungle.

The route leads through a classic pointed Mayan arch to the Cuadrángulo de las Monjas (Nuns' Quadrangle), so named by the Spaniards on account of its rows of cells and the delicacy of its carved façades. The structures, called simply the North, South, East, and West Buildings, are arranged around a broad courtyard and are noted for their symmetry and elegant proportions. Decorations and carvings of the rain god Chac appear on some of the outer walls.

From the Nuns' Quadrangle you will pass the small Juego de Pelota (Ball Court) and Casa de las Tortugas (House of Turtles) before arriving at the impressive Palacio del Gobernador (Governor's Palace), which stands on a massive platform. Considered an architectural masterpiece of the period, it is noted for its exquisite façade and the geometric decorations in the frieze. Other structures of note include the

Archaeologists have yet to ascertain the original use of the 74-room Nuns' Quadrangle

Gran Pirámide (Great Pyramid) and the
Palomar (Dovecot).
*76km south of Mérida. Open: daily
8am–5pm. Admission charge (Sundays and
holidays free). Sound and light presentations:
every evening, weather permitting (Spanish
7pm, English 9pm). Local bus from Mérida
or organized excursion. Admission charge.*

Surrounding sites

South of Uxmal are several smaller
Mayan sites well worth visiting. About
21km southeast on the R261 are the ruins
of Kabah. The most striking building is
the one known as the Codz-Pop, which
features some 250 masks of the rain god
Chac. Codz-Pop (rolled-up mat) refers to
the odd trunk-like noses of the masks.
Across the road stands a solitary Mayan
arch.

Farther along the R261, a left turn
leads to Sayil, Xlapak, and Labná in the
Puuc Archaeological Zone, whose style is
characterized by plain walls with
elaborate stucco and stone ornamentation
above.

Sayil is dominated by the splendid
Palacio (Palace), embellished with *chac*
masks, columns, and a pair of reptiles
flanking an upside-down figure.

Xlapak's main building is a contrast of
subtlety and splendid exuberance,
including more long-nosed masks of the
god Chac.

Labná is known for its monumental
arch, the most profusely decorated in all
Mayan architecture.

Return to the R261 and continue
south. At Hopelchén, take the R180 to
Campeche and turn left at Edzná. The
most impressive feature of this well-
restored site is the Templo de los Cinco
Pisos (Temple of the Five Levels).
*Sites – open daily 8am–5pm; admission
charge (Sundays and holidays free).*

UXMAL

SITE PLAN
1 Juego de Pelota
2 Casa de las Tortugas
3 Palomar
4 Cuadrángulo de las Monjas
5 Templo de Cementario
6 Grupo de las Columnas
7 Grupo Noroeste
8 Grupo Oeste
9 Templo de los Ciempiés
10 Templo de los Falos

Villahermosa

*A*midst the steamy jungles and swamplands of Tabasco lies Villahermosa, the state capital. Important oil discoveries in the 1970s, and agricultural development in the region transformed the area into a fast-growing boom town. This is *macho* country, with great strapping ranchers seen about town (a lone woman here may well find herself the object of too much attention).

While its modern, brash image may not appeal to some, the city offers some pleasant diversions. You can stroll about the busy pedestrianized area downtown and onto the Grijalva River, where the *malecón* (promenade) invites a meander along its banks. Music relayed through "singing lampposts" adds a rather charming touch. Boat trips along the Grijalva provide a glimpse of typical Tabasco jungle terrain (the ride lasts about 2 hours, and lunch is served on board). For many tourists traveling by air, Villahermosa serves merely as an overnight stop before visiting the Mayan ruins at Palenque, one of Mexico's top attractions (see pages 104–5). However, there are two museums that should on no account be missed.

CICOM

This is the acronym for the Centro de Investigaciones de las Culturas Olmeca y Maya, an anthropological research center emphasizing the Olmec and Maya civilizations. Within this huge cultural complex is the Carlos Pellicer Camara Regional Museum, where you can see a magnificent collection of pieces from many of the pre-Hispanic cultures. *Calle Ocampo (on riverbank). Tel: 12–32–00. Open: daily 9am–8pm. Admission charge (Sundays and holidays free).*

Olmec head, La Venta: a party of school children see a piece of their history

PARQUE MUSEO DE LA VENTA

Back in the 1950s, Olmec sculptures were brought to this unique open-air park museum from the archaeological site of La Venta, 95km away, where oil fields were being developed. Stone sculpture was the hallmark of Olmec art. Some 30 items are displayed in a jungle setting very much like their place of origin. The main fascination is with three colossal basalt-stone heads, each weighing as much as 20 tons. (More such monolith heads can be seen in the Museums of Anthropology in Jalapa, Veracruz, and Mexico City.)

In the park is also a small zoo. There are many free-roaming animals, and you may well come across monkeys, deer, the odd tapir, and perhaps a family of coatimundis (close relatives of the racoon), which appear at the first sign of any food. Remember to use insect repellent.

Boulevard Ruiz Cortines, near Paseo Tabasco. Tel: 15–22–28. Open: Tuesday to Sunday 9am–5pm. Monday 8am–4pm. Admission charge.

THE OLMECS

The "people from the land of rubber" (in Náhuatl) are seen as the forerunners of all pre-Columbian civilizations. They developed a culture around the Gulf Coast that flourished between about 1200 BC and 400 BC. These were the first known people to build pyramid bases for temples, which remained as basic mounds of earth. They also developed a numerical system and glyphic script.

The centers of the Olmec civilization were San Lorenzo, which was destroyed around 900 BC, La Venta (in Tabasco), and Tres Zapotes, located west of the Tuxtlas. The Olmecs worked with jade and precious stones, carved stone altars, sculptures and stelae, and are known for the great monolithic basalt heads found at these sites. Thought to represent prominent leaders, they are on display in various museums, including La Venta.

Nearby

The most westerly of the ancient Mayan cities was Comalcalco, 60km northwest of Villahermosa, which flourished between AD 800 and 1250. The site was not built of stone, but of sun-baked bricks and mortar made of sand, clay, and ground oyster shells.

The Gran Acropolis features some large, finely detailed stucco masks.

Open: daily 9am–4:30pm. Admission charge (Sundays and holidays are free).

Villahermosa is 860km southeast of Mexico City. Information office: Paseo Tabasco 1504. Tel: 16-28-90. Flights from Mexico City and other domestic destinations.

Olmec carving, La Venta

Northern Mexico

*T*he area loosely called Northern Mexico stretches from the Gulf of Grande)
California, in the west, to the Gulf of Mexico in the east. The Río Bravo (or
Río forms the greater part of thecountry's border with the States.

NORTHERN MEXICO

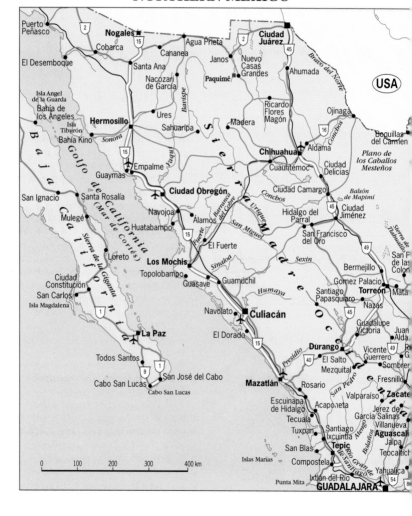

This is a region of arid lands, lofty mountains, and plateaus. The Sierra Madre Oriental and Sierra Madre Occidental run parallel to the eastern and western coasts, respectively. Between the ranges is a high plain

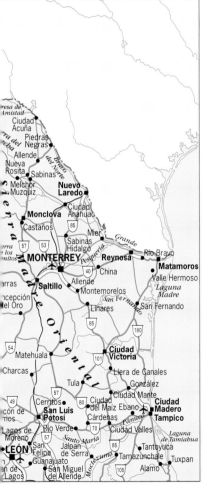

Only the hardiest plants adapt to desert life

where Mexico's major cities lie.

Sonora, in the north-western corner, is characterized by deserts, populated largely by cacti, yet with a stark, haunting beauty. The west coast, with its cliffs, beaches, coastal plains, and jungle, also offers excellent sportfishing.

The north is renowned for its cattle raising, and huge ranches are to be found in Sonora, Chihuahua, and around San Luis Potosí, farther south. It is also a rich mining area, and serves as the base for an increasing number of *maquiladoras* (assembly plants for U.S. products). Monterrey is an important industrial center and a major producer of beer.

Although not tourist country, many of its attractions are unique. Giant saguaro and other cacti stand sentinel across the great Sonoran deserts. The countryside around Monterrey and Durango is lonely and wild, suited to the many Westerns filmed there. A fascinating rail journey through the Barranca del Cobre (Copper Canyon), in Chihuahua offers side-trips deep down into the canyons, and a glimpse of the Tarahumara Indians who inhabit the area (see pages 138–9).

Chihuahua

*C*apital of the largest and one of the richest states in Mexico, Chihuahua is a major agricultural, cattle, and industrial center, with the *maquiladora* industry (assembly plants for American companies) now also big business. The place exudes an air of affluence, with a noticeable influence from north of the border. Modern buildings contrast with old traditional homes, and well-heeled ranchers are seen about town. Chihuahua is the starting or finishing point for the famous Copper Canyon railway trip (see pages 138–9).

Historically, the region has seen much turbulence. The Spaniards expended a lot of time and effort to settle the area, which was continuously under attack from the Apache and Comanche Indians. These tribes continued to cause problems in the town's development after silver mining began at the start of the 18th century. Independence hero Father Miguel Hidalgo and some of his band were captured and executed here in 1811. The town was occupied for short periods by U.S. troops during the 1846–8 war with North America, and the War of Intervention (1862–6). In 1913, during the Mexican Revolution, the legendary Pancho Villa established his headquarters here, capturing the town by disguising his men as peasants going to market.

Chihuahua's splendid cathedral: its completion was delayed by continual Indian raids

Catedral Metropolitana

Dominating the main square is the twin-towered Catedral. Completed in 1826, it has a magnificent baroque façade and a rich interior of gold and marble.

Plaza de Armas. Open: weekdays 10am–2pm, 4–6pm. Admission charge.

Museo de la Revolución "Quinta Luz"

Also known simply as Casa Villa (Villa's House), this is the former home and headquarters of the notorious, heroic Pancho Villa. Photographs, furniture, weapons, and relics evoke the atmosphere of the Revolution, and recall the bold life of the bandit-turned-general. Most dramatic of the exhibits is perhaps the bullet-holed Dodge car in which he and his companions were assassinated in 1923. The museum was established after his death by his widow, Luz Corral, who looked after it until her death in 1981.

Calle Décima. Tel: 16–29–58. Open: daily 10am–1pm, 3–7pm. Admission charge.

Palacio Del Gobierno

The Governor's Palace is where Father Hidalgo was shot early on in the Independence War. At the Fatherland's Altar, built on the very spot of his execution, flickers an eternal flame.

Opposite Plaza Hidalgo. Tel: 10–63–24. Open: daily 8am–8pm.

Surroundings

Casas Grandes, also known as Paquimé, is the most important archaeological site in northern Mexico. Although evidence suggests a much earlier occupation, its culture is believed to have flourished between AD 900 and 1100. In the 14th century, the place was destroyed by nomadic tribes. The site includes the adobe ruins of communal housing units, underground channels that supplied running water, a large ball court, and a central plaza.

270km northwest of Chihuahua. Open: daily 10am–5pm. Admission charge.

Wear a hat while visiting Paquimé, the major trading center of the North from AD 1000–1200

Located west of Chihuahua is Cuauhtémoc, an important cattle and farming town. The surrounding area is inhabited by a Mennonite colony, which produces cheese, meats, and apples. It offers an interesting visit to observe the way of life of these people, who came here in the early 1920s (see pages 138–9).

105km west of Chihuahua.

Chihuahua is 375km south of Ciudad Juárez. Information office: Palacio de Gobierno (central patio), Plaza Hidalgo.. Tel: 10–10–77. Flights from Mexico City, other domestic and U.S. destinations. Regular bus connections from Mexico City and U.S. border towns. Trains to Ciudad Juárez, Mexico City, and Los Mochis (through the Copper Canyon).

The film sets of many a Hollywood western can be visited near Durango

DURANGO

Durango flourished when gold, silver, and other minerals were found here in the 18th and 19th centuries. Designated a national historic monument, the state capital has attractive colonial architecture.

Casa de los Condes de Súchil

This 18th-century residence has a façade of carved stone; inside, an enormous Moorish arch leads to the main patio with its double arcade.
5 de Febrero 32.

Catedral

Begun in the late 17th century, this structure is primarily baroque in style. Note the pretty ironwork on the left tower, and the finely carved images on the choir stalls.
North side of the main square.

Palacio de Gobierno

This 18th-century Governor's Palace originally belonged to a wealthy miner. Its colonial-style arcades are decorated with murals depicting Durango's history.
Zaragoza and 5 de Febrero.

Villa del Oeste

A special attraction for film fans is the old sets remaining from the time when Westerns were produced *en masse* here. Two "cowboy towns" seen in many a John Wayne film, 14km north of the city, can be visited on organized tours on weekends.
Contact your hotel or local tourist office to arrange a visit.

598km north of Guadalajara. Information office: Hidalgo Sur 408. Tel: 1–21–39. Buses from Mexico City, Guadalajara, and Mazatlán. Also connected by rail, but slow.

MONTERREY

Monterrey is Nuevo León's state capital and Mexico's third largest city. It sprawls over a large valley dominated by the imposing Cerro de la Silla (Saddle Mountain), the symbol of the city. Although a modern industrial center, it still retains sections of colonial charm, with narrow streets and cool, inviting courtyards. The Gran Plaza is an unusually spacious square, containing government buildings, fountains, sculptures, and theaters, all exhibiting a contrast of styles.

Cervercería Cuauhtémoc

Monterrey is famous for its production of beer. The Cuauhtémoc Brewery, founded towards the end of the last century,

developed into one of the major beer enterprises in Mexico.
Avenida Universidad 2202. Tel: 72–48–94. Open: Tuesday to Sunday 9:30am–5pm, weekends 10am–6pm. Tours by request. Tel: 75–22–00 to confirm.

Museo de Arte Contemporáneo

Known as MARCO, this well-designed building hosts outstanding temporary exhibits of contemporary art.
Gran Plaza. Tel: 42–48–20/30. Open: Tuesday and Thursday to Saturday 11am–7pm. Wednesday and Sunday 11am–9pm. Admission charge.

Museo de Historia Mexicana

This new museum gives an insight into the history of Mexico's 1910 revolution, presented in modern style. A river walk, cafés, and boat ride add to the attraction.
Dr Coss 445 Sur. Tel: 345–98–98. Open: Tuesday to Thursday 11am–7pm. Friday to Sunday 11am–8pm. Admission charge.

Surroundings

Impressive natural attractions include the Grutas de García (García Caves) 45km west, with stalagmite and stalactite formations, a subterranean lake, and 16 lighted caverns. The Cola de Caballo (Horsetail Falls), 40km south, has a wooded path beside a stream which cuts through a ravine to reach the base of the falls. The stunning Cañon de Huasteca (Huasteca Canyon), 10km south of town, has sheer rock walls rising out of the landscape to pierce the sky; and the Chipinque Mesa, 19km southwest of town, is a beauty spot offering marvelous views, popular for picnics and camping.

963km north of Mexico City. Information office: Calle Padre Mier and Dr. Coss. Tel: 345–08–70. Flights from Mexico City, other Mexican destinations, and the United States. Bus and rail.

Neptune emerges from a Monterrey fountain

SAN LUIS POTOSÍ

Situated right in the heart of cattle-ranching country, this old mining town has a very Mexican flavor. Although not on the tourist track, it has considerable charm and some fine buildings, mostly clustered near the heart of the city. After silver and gold were found in the area at the end of the 16th century, San Luis became one of the most important towns in Mexico. Evidence of the town's past wealth can be seen in its fine colonial buildings and attractive squares.

Catedral

The 17th-century twin-towered cathedral has an impressive baroque façade, with a porch adorned by statues of the twelve Apostles. Its interior is composed of various styles.
Plaza de Armas.

Museo Regional Potosino

Housed in the former Franciscan convent, this regional museum contains archaeological pieces, sculptures and vessels, wrought-iron work, and a fine Churriqueresque chapel upstairs.
Galeana 450. Tel: 1251–85/75–21. Open: Tuesday to Friday 10am–1pm, 3–6pm, weekends 10am–noon. Admission charge.

Templo del Carmen

Perhaps the most interesting of the city's churches, this Carmelite building is noted for its baroque façade, grand tiled dome, and richly adorned interior.
Plaza del Carmen.

Templo de San Francisco

The interior of this 17th-century church has scenes from the life of St. Francis, as well as an unusual chandelier shaped like a ship, suspended over the apse, and said to have been donated by a shipwreck survivor. The sacristy is outstanding.
Plaza San Francisco. Open: 7am–2pm, 4–9pm. Closed: Wednesday and Sunday.

417km north of Mexico City. Information office: Carranza 325. Tel: 12–99–39. Bus connections to Mexico City, Monterrey, and León.

ZACATECAS

Set at high altitude, in hilly terrain, at the foot of the Cerro de la Bufa, the state capital is surrounded by agricultural and ranching land. It dates from the 16th century, when Spaniards discovered rich deposits of silver, copper, and zinc nearby. Great quantities of silver were shipped to Spain, and the town flourished for the next three centuries. Elegant colonial mansions and churches bear testimony to this affluence. Today, this picturesque city of pink-stone houses is still a center for silver mining, with a colonial heritage still rarely touched by tourism. Its narrow cobblestone streets, alleyways, and handsome buildings, make this a rewarding town to explore on foot.

Catedral

The cathedral stands out as one of Mexico's finest examples of the Churriquesque style. Its rose-colored façade is adorned with elaborate carvings, crowned by a figure of Christ flanked by the twelve Apostles. The interior, by contrast, is in plain neo-classical style.
Plaza de Armas.

Cerro de la Bufa

The summit of the hill that dominates Zacatecas can best be reached by the *teleférico*, the Swiss-made aerial cable car that climbs sedately to the chapel at the top, a renowned pilgrimage site. From here there are magnificent views of the entire city.

Museum on Pancho Villa – open: Tuesday to Sunday 10am–5pm. Admission charge.

Mina del Edén

Mini trains tour the abandoned 16th-century Eden Mine; the adventurous can cross a hanging bridge over one of the shafts. By night, the place is a disco.

Northeast of town, near the hospital. Tel: 2–30–02. Open: daily 10am–6pm. Admission charge.

Museo Pedro Coronel

Housed in a former Jesuit monastery, the museum contains a fine collection of artworks donated by the Zacatecan artist Pedro Coronel.

Avenida Fernando Villalpando, at Plaza Santo Domingo. Tel: 2–80–21. Open: Friday to Wednesday 10am–2pm and 4–7pm. Admission charge.

Palacio de Gobierno

This handsome 18th-century building, now the City Hall, once served as a residence for some of the Zacatecan nobility.

Worth seeing are the attractive courtyard and historical mural.

East side of Plaza de Armas.

Templo de Santo Domingo

St. Dominic's Church, the richest in Zacatecas, dates back to the mid-18th century. It was built on massive foundations that compensate for the uneven terrain.

Calle Codina.

613km north of Mexico City. Information office: Avenida Hidalgo and Callejón del Santero. Tel: 4–03–93. Flights from Mexico City, Tijuana, and Los Angeles. Buses from Mexico City and Guadalajara.

Cathedral bell-tower in Zacatecas

Baja California

*S*ome 20 million years ago, seismic upheavals along the notorious San Andréas Fault caused a narrow finger of land to separate from the mainland of Mexico. The waters of the Pacific filled the gap – now called the Gulf of California, or the Mar de Cortés – and formed the long peninsula known as Baja (Lower) California.

From the U.S. border in the north to its southernmost point, Baja California is some 1,300km long. It averages about 90km across and, at its widest, is only 193km. The area was originally inhabited by various Indian groups, and a number of prehistoric cave paintings have been found. Among the most significant are those around San Ignacio.

Hernán Cortés first came here in 1535 to what became La Paz, but it took time and effort to settle the region. Jesuit priests were sent here in the 17th century, and began establishing missions. They worked in good faith and gradually succeeded in converting the Indians to Christianity. During the 19th century, foreigners bought land and established large ranches. Fishing began in earnest, and is big business today.

Often simply called Baja, the peninsula is divided at the 28th Parallel into two states, Baja California Norte (North) and Baja California Sur (South).

Two high ranges run down its length: the Sierra San Pedro Martír, with pine and oak forests, in the northern half, and the Sierra de la Giganta in the south. The central region is dominated by the Desierto Vizcaíno (Vizcaíno Desert), with landscapes of giant cacti, cirios, and wind-polished boulders. The north is more agricultural, with valleys devoted to vineyards, olive groves, cotton and wheat, while the south is characterized by lush vegetation, fine sandy beaches, and rugged rock formations against a warm emerald sea. Although tourism is growing, Baja still offers great untouched expanses of natural beauty in a climate that is reliably dry and pleasant all year round.

Baja California wine country: the vineyards of venerable Santo Tomás, south of Ensenada

BAJA CALIFORNIA

Stern countenances of historical personages look out at the Plaza Civica in Ensenada

BAJA CALIFORNIA NORTE

ENSENADA

This delightful, busy seaport is the nearest major beach resort to Tijuana, and a long-time favorite with both Mexicans and Southern Californians. It offers fine sandy beaches, good deep-sea fishing, sailing, surfing, and a casino. The surrounding area is wine country, and visits to the wineries of Cavas Valmar or Bodegas de Santo Tomás, the oldest on the peninsula, can be arranged (ask at your hotel or the tourist office). Crafts from all over Mexico – silver, pottery, and *serapes* (colorful woven blankets) – are priced extremely competitively.

Some 35km southwest of Ensenada is Cabo Punta de la Banda, where the mountains drop straight into the sea. Here, over the centuries, the pounding surf has formed a hole through which the waves crash with tremendous power, forcing the water up to a great height. The loud, peculiar noise it makes gave it its name, La Bufadora (The Snorting One or The Blow Hole).
108km south of Tijuana. Information office: Blvd. Costera 1477. Tel: 72–30–22. Car or bus to Tijuana, Mexicali, and other centers.

MEXICALI

Mexicali, capital of Baja California Norte, is a busy border town orientated more towards business than tourism. However, there are a couple of places worth a visit, especially the museum.

Museo del Estado

Exhibits depict Baja's archaeology, history, culture, and missions.
Avenida Reforma. Tel: 52–57–17. Open: Tuesday to Saturday 9am–6pm, Sunday 10am–2pm. Admission charge.

On the U.S. border, 169km east of Tijuana. Information office: Calle Calafia. Tel: 56–10–72. Flights from Mexico City, other Mexican and U.S. destinations. Bus connections to Mexico City and other Mexican destinations. Rail services to Mexico City and Guadalajara.

SAN FELIPE

From a picturesque fishing and shrimping port, San Felipe has grown into a favorite beach resort for North Americans. It lies on the Gulf of California, with majestic rocky mountains and inland desert for a backdrop. Its long sandy beaches bustle with cars and campers on weekends and throughout the tourist season. Condominiums and hotels line the waterfront and plans continue for a new marina development just outside the town. San Felipe is also popular for sport fishing.

200km south of Mexicali. Information office: Mar de Cortés and Manzanillo (tel: 7–11–55). Buses to Mexicali and Ensenada.

TIJUANA

Formerly a notorious border town, Tijuana has largely cleaned up its act and no longer merits its "Sin City" image. A better nickname might be "Fun City." A 30-minute drive or so from San Diego leads to another world – of color, noise, chaos, and fun. According to statistics, Tijuana receives more U.S. visitors annually than any other foreign city in the world. Discount prices in this duty-free zone attract hordes of day shoppers. Tijuana offers many sporting attractions such as jai alai, bullfights, horse and dog racing, rodeos, and baseball. Many

visitors cross the border just to enjoy the restaurants, bars, and nightclubs.

Mexitlán Theme Park

Large complex featuring models of Mexico's finest pre-Hispanic and colonial monuments, along with regional folk music.

Avenida Ocampo. Tel: 38–41–01. Open: Wednesday to Sunday 10am–10pm (5pm in winter). Admission charge.

Scale models at the Mexitlán theme park

Tijuana Centro Cultural

This attractively designed modern complex contains a history museum, temporary exhibits, and local handicrafts, in addition to the spectacular Omnimax movie cinema.

Paseo de los Héroes and Avenida Independencia. Tel: 84–11–117. Open: daily 9am–8pm. Admission charge.

On the U.S. border, 25km south of San Diego. Information office: Third Level of Plaza Patria, on Boulevard Díaz Ordaz. Tel: 81–94–92. Flights from Mexico City, other Mexican destinations, Los Angeles, and other U.S. destinations. Bus from Mexico City and other Mexican destinations.

This tame zebra is actually a painted donkey!

WHALE WATCHING

Every autumn thousands of California gray whales migrate south from Alaska's Bering Strait to central Baja's Pacific coast. Hunted nearly to extinction by 1946, but now dramatically recovered in numbers, these stately giants – as long as 15m and weighing between 20 and 40 tons when mature – take two to three months to make the 9,500km journey. Once there, in the warm, tranquil lagoons, they court, mate, snort, and cavort in an amorous free-for-all, while calving mothers give birth in shallower waters to the young conceived the previous year.

Each baby is born weighing 750–1,000kg and measuring about 5m long; suckling its mother's rich milk (53 percent fat), the calf doubles its weight and adds another meter to its length by the end of the winter. Adults begin heading back north in March, with the calves – being strenuously trained by their mothers in the mouth of the lagoon – following on as late as May or June.

Looking "through the keyhole" at the grey whales' intimate domestic life is an intriguing and ever more popular pastime. The main whale sanctuaries where these giant mammals display their antics are Scammon's Lagoon (named for the Maine whaler who found the breeding ground in 1857), Laguna San Ignacio, and Magdalena Bay. The first is 40km from Guerrero Negro, a town just below the border that divides Baja into north and

Images of man approaching nature with care: even in playful mood, these massive creatures have a great dignity that commands respect

Scammon's Lagoon, also known as Ojo de Liebre (Eye of the Hare), was declared a Gray Whale Natural Park; this and its sister lagoon at Guerrero Negro were the first such sanctuaries in the world. Laguna San Ignacio, some 200km farther south, which services one of the world's largest salt evaporation works; Magdalena Bay is the best place to see them, since it is the most accessible of the three from La Paz, and is geared up for whale watching. In 1960, south, gained similar status in 1979.

For the closest possible encounter, boat trips on the lagoons can be arranged locally; for the more timid, a pair of binoculars on the shore will do nicely.

Loreto's mission church sent forth the friars who founded the chain of California missions

regular ferry services to the mainland, improved airport facilities, and a paved Transpeninsular Highway ensured its revival.

In spite of much growth, there are enough arched doorways and flower-filled patios to keep the graceful character of old La Paz. Many businesses, especially in summer, observe the traditional afternoon *siesta*. By night the zócalo, brilliantly illuminated with old pebble-glass globes, is a rare sight. The Anthropological Museum has good displays of the region's geology, history, prehistory, and folklore (Ignacio Altimirano and 5 de Mayo). A series of beautiful beaches stretching up the coast offers good snorkeling, fishing, and some stunning sunsets.

1,384km south of Tijuana. Information office: Paseo Alvaro Obregón 2130. Tel: 2–11–90. Anthropolgical museum – Cinco de Mayo and Altamirano. Tel: 2–01–62. Open: daily 8am–6pm. Free. Flights from Mexico City, other Mexican destinations and international flights from the United States.

BAJA CALIFORNIA SUR
LA PAZ

La Paz (Peace) has a pleasant *malecón* (seafront promenade), beach, and a busy port; its free port status means there are plenty of bargains to be had. Large passenger and car ferries depart for Mazatlán and Topolobampo on the mainland from Pichilingue, 16km north.

The waters of La Paz once supported a thriving pearl-fishing business (John Steinbeck's story *The Pearl* is said to have been based on a tale he heard here in 1941). However, in 1940 a mysterious epidemic wiped out the oysters, and all but killed off the town as well – until

LORETO

The first permanent settlement in Baja California was founded here by the Jesuits in 1697. Loreto became the peninsula's first capital, but lost this status in 1830 after the town was devastated by a hurricane. Time seems to have stood still in this historic town. It has a few shady squares and a pleasant *malecón* (seafront promenade). The project for a tourist developement, south of Loreto, has produced a new golf course, with plans in the cards for additional accommodations.

Misión de Nuestra Señora de Loreto
This well-restored, early 18th-century
mission church on the zócalo has a small
adjoining museum, the Museo de los
Misiones, which depicts local history,
culture, and mission activities.
*Zócalo. Museum – open: Wednesday to
Sunday 9am–4pm.*

*356km north of La Paz. Air connections
from Mexico City, Tijuana, and Los
Angeles. Buses from Tijuana and La Paz.*

LOS CABOS
Los Cabos (The Capes) is the name given
to the southernmost area of the peninsula,
divided into the two resorts of San José
del Cabo and Cabo San Lucas. The area
has seen considerable development over
recent years, and a variety of attractive
hotels are strung along the stretch of
coastline known as the "corridor," which
is characterized by long sandy beaches,
dramatic rock formations, and coves. The
setting of desert, mountains, and sea,
combined with good fishing, aquatic
sports, and several top-class golf courses,
gives the area a special appeal.

Cabo San Lucas
Cabo San Lucas – once a sheltering place
for treasure ships from the Orient, as well
as pirates – is a lively resort with an ever-
increasing supply of hotels, restaurants,
and night spots. The harbor is a busy
spot, with its large fishing fleet and open-
air market. It is internationally renowned
for year-round sport-fishing; charter
arrangements can be made on the
waterfront, or through many of the hotels.
Distinctive black coral jewelry is made
and sold at the regional arts center at the
cruise liner dock. Sandy beaches, blue-
green seas, and a coastline of volcanic
formations offer many other attractions.

There is good swimming, surfing, scuba
diving, and snorkeling, as well as water-
skiing, parasailing, windsurfing, and
volleyball. Golf and tennis are also
widely available.

Visitors should take a boat trip to the
striking rock formation known as El Arco
(The Arch). The area is rich in marine
life and favored by divers. At the point
where the Pacific meets the Gulf lies the
secluded Playa de Amor (Lover's Beach),
popular for swimming and picnics.

Waves pound against rock at Cabo San Lucas

San José del Cabo
This small trading and tourist center has
a shady main square, shops, a few hotels,
and a mission-style church – a place to
visit rather than to stay in. The real
holiday area is the hotel zone that has
developed within the community.
Hotels, condominiums, and villas stretch
along the coast.

*Los Cabos is located at the south tip of the
peninsula, 216km south of La Paz. Flights
from Mexico City, other Mexican and
U.S. destinations. Bus connections to La
Paz. Cabo San Lucas is also a port of call
for ocean liners.*

MULEGÉ

This delightful little tropical oasis, with its hilltop mission church, lies on an estuary a few kilometers from the Gulf. With its narrow streets, thatched roofs, and date palms first planted by the Jesuits, it has great charm and is a popular stopover for travelers exploring the peninsula. South of town, a short distance away, are some attractive beaches along Bahía Concepción. There are charter fishing trips to nearby islands, and good diving and snorkeling. Guided excursions are available to see some ancient cave paintings near San Baltazar and San Patricio; San Borjita Cave contains an interesting collection of petroglyphs, but is less accessible.
495km north of La Paz. Buses from Tijuana to La Paz stop here.

SANTA ROSALÍA

Ever since its founding in 1855 by a French-owned copper-mining company, Santa Rosalía has retained a certain Gallic flavor, its picturesque wooden houses and long verandas distinctly influenced by French colonial style. The focal point of the town is the harbor, which serves as a terminal for regular car ferries across to Guaymas on the mainland. During World War I, Germany's Pacific sailing fleet was interned here for the duration. The Palacio Municipal is a fine example of French architecture. The most impressive landmark in the town, however, is the 19th-century church, thought to have been designed by Gustave Eiffel (of Eiffel Tower fame), and constructed of prefabricated galvanized iron in France and shipped over to Mexico. Rail enthusiasts will like the relics of the meter-gauge steam-powered railway that served the mines and smelter before the turn of the century. One locomotive can be seen in the town center, and more equipment is displayed outdoors, about 500m north along the highway. The nearby beaches of Santa María and San Lucas offer good swimming.
65km north of Mulegé. Buses from Tijuana and La Paz.

In a departure from the usual Spanish influence, Santa Rosalía shows French style

GETTING AWAY FROM IT ALL

"It was the jungle, but domesticated; a vast essay in tropical landscape gardening, richly, romantically beautiful."

ALDOUS HUXLEY
Beyond the Mexique Bay, 1934

Getting Away from It All

A country the size of Mexico is bound to offer many exciting and diverse opportunities for those who seek something out of the ordinary. Lakeside resorts, spas, and beautiful national parks beckon to those who seek peace and tranquility. For the more adventurous, there is much to explore. Ecotourism, a new concept in Mexico, promotes nature-related travel with a low impact on the environment. An increasing number of tours are organized to more remote parts of Mexico, with visits to wildlife and nature reserves.

CAVES AND *CENOTES*

Dotted about the countryside are a number of caves (*grutas*) with stunning stalactite and stalagmite formations. Always take a guide, or join a tour.

Northeast of Taxco are the Grutas de Cacahuamilpa (Cacahuamilpa Caves), which are noted for their spectacular rock formations. In the vicinity, you can also visit the nearby Grutas de Estrella (Star Grottoes) and the Grutas de Juxtlahuaca (Juxtlahuaca Caves), southeast of Chilpancingo. The Cocoría Caves, 56km south of Villahermosa, are also known for their striking limestone formations.

The Yucatán is honeycombed by caves, *cenotes* (sinkholes) and underground rivers, which are opening up exciting new opportunities for diving.

Never explore on your own, however, and heed warning signs.

Among the region's most impressive caves are the Grutas de Loltún (Loltún Grottoes) south of Mérida, which contain Mayan wall paintings and artifacts; Calcehtok Cave farther west features lofty vaults and underground streams. In the Balancanché Cave, 5km east of Chichén Itzá, there is a small lake and more Mayan relics.

Some of the *cenotes* offer excellent snorkeling, or merely a refreshing swim in an unusual setting. Among the most attractive are those at Dzitnup near Valladolid, Chen-Ha southwest of Mérida, and Xtogil, some 20km east of Chichén Itzá. At Xcaret (see page 97), south of Cancún, an underground river passes through impressive submerged caverns that served as sacred *cenotes*. By the Cenote Azul on the shores of Laguna Bacalar, north of Chetumal, you can swim or enjoy excellent seafood at the *palapa*-roofed restaurant, while watching young boys dive into waters of stunning clarity. The most famous of them all is the Cenote Sagrado in Chichén Itzá (see pages 98–9), where virgins are said to have been sacrificed to the rain god. This one is not for swimming!

In Yucatán, mysteriously evocative waters ripple in a sacred *cenote* at Dzibilchaltun

Sturdy pillar-like Joshua palms pose jauntily against the desert sky of Nuevo León

Ask your hotel or contact the local tourist office for more information. Visits to some of the grottoes and *cenotes* are included in organized excursions.

DESERTS AND JUNGLES

The desertlands of northern Mexico and Baja California can provide the perfect, unexpected refuge. The great Sonoran Desert in the northwest, extending well into the United States, offers Arizona-type vistas, with giant cacti silhouetted against a brilliant blue sky. Baja California offers an appealing contrast of desert, sea, and mountains; in the peninsula's interior there is some wild terrain that will challenge your determination to arrive. The Cataviña Natural Park, south of El Rosario, offers some of the most bizarre scenery in Baja: giant boulders among acres of weirdly shaped cirio trees and great cardon cacti.

A hiking trip through a tropical jungle is the stuff of many people's fantasies. In the jungle regions of southeastern Mexico, you can easily combine such a trek with a visit to Mayan ruins or other centers. Archaeological sites like Palenque (see pages 104–5), Bonampak, and Yaxchilán (see page 103) are buried deep in the jungle. Kohunlich, near Chetumal, is surrounded by massive kapok trees and magnificent palms; Becán, Chicanná, and Balankú among many other archaeological sites in Campeche, offer walks into the engulfing vegetation. For those who don't wish to venture beyond an urban setting, the open-air museum of La Venta in Villahermosa (see page 113), and the excellent Zoomat in Tuxtla Gutiérrez (see page 159) are both in exotic jungle surroundings.

Interesting jungle excursions and riding expeditions are organized from Puerto Vallarta (see pages 88–9) and from Yelapa, across the bay. Do not venture into the jungle without a guide, stick to marked trails, and bring plenty of powerful insect repellent!

HIKING AND CLIMBING

If you are looking for a relaxed walk in the countryside, you can find this in any of the national parks, where marked paths lead through beautiful surroundings. From Mexico City, you can make day trips to the national parks of Desierto de los Leones, Ajusco, Lagunas de Zempoala, Izta-Popo, and Nevado de Toluca, which offer cool pine forests, lakes, and fresh mountain air.

For dedicated hikers who wish to get off the beaten track, there are countless possibilities depending on your interests. The Barranca del Cobre (Copper Canyon) region in northwestern Mexico offers awesome landscapes and splendid isolation. (Treks down into the canyons should not be attempted without the services of a local guide.) In the highlands of Chiapas, following the trails from one village to another gives a fascinating glimpse of local life. As a contrast, the flat scrublands of the Yucatán make for pleasant walking, and can be combined with visits to lesser-known Mayan ruins and wildlife refuges. For those with time to spare, it is even possible to walk right around the peninsula of Baja California – it has been done!

Mountaineering, in the true sense of the word, is limited in Mexico. Very little rock climbing is possible owing to the unsuitable texture of the rocks at high altitudes. The three tallest peaks in Mexico – Orizaba, Popocatépetl, and Iztaccíhuatl – are often climbed, but require a great deal of fitness and stamina, if not first-class mountaineering skills (see pages 74–5). La Malinche and Nevado de Colima volcanoes are also popular mountain climbs.

For more information contact: CAM (Club Alpino Méxicano), Córdoba 234–2, 06700 México DF, tel: 574–96–83, or Club de Exploraciones de México, Juan Mateos 146, México DF, tel: 578–57–30.

LAKES, LAGOONS, AND RIVERS

The shores of some of Mexico's lakes, each with its own distinctive personality, are havens of peace and quiet. The largest is Lake Chapala. The town of Chapala (see page 52) has a lively promenade of bars, restaurants, and *mariachi* bands. For a calmer existence, try the quaint little lakeside villages of Ajijic or Jocotepec, which attract the artistic set.

Lake Pátzcuaro (see page 61), southwest of Morelia in neighboring Michoacán, has a much quieter appeal. You can take a launch across to the curious cone-shaped island of Janitzio, or explore some of the tiny Tarascan

Hikers in Chiapas carry water in backpacks

A lazy day at the lakeside of Catemaco, formed in the crater of an old volcano

RIVERS AND RAFTING
A boat trip on the Grijalva River through the Cañon del Sumidero (Sumidero Canyon) is a thrilling experience, offering dramatic scenery as it passes between walls of sheer rock edging closer and rising to great heights (see page 103). Boarding points are from Cuaharé or Chiapa de Corzo (east of Tuxtla Gutiérrez). Exciting river-boat trips into jungle hinterland can also be taken from Villahermosa and Tenocique (Tabasco), and Champotón (Campeche). Ecogrupos de México, Insurgentes Sur 1971, Mexico City (tel: 661–91–21) offers tours including boat trips through the Sumidero Canyon and on the Usumacinta river, around the ruins of Yaxchilán (see page 103). White-water rafting on Veracruz's navigable rivers (June to October) is fast growing in popularity. Rafting tours are offered by Expediciones México Verde (tel: 255–44–00 in Mexico City).

communities around the lakeside.

South of Mexico City is a lovely region of lakes and forests contained within Parque Nacional Lagunas de Zempoala (Zempoala National Park). A little farther, near Cuernavaca, is Lake Tequesquitengo, which offers boating and aquatic sports (weekdays are normally quiet). For something unusual, try the crater lake of Catemaco, 10km southeast of San Andrés Tuxtla in Veracruz; boat trips can be made to an islet inhabited by a colony of monkeys. The area is known for its witchcraft, and people come here to have a spell cast or a curse removed!

In the Yucatán are some enchanting lagoons, such as Xel-Há south of Cancún (see page 97), or the Chancanab lagoon on Cozumel island (see page 97). Most spectacular are the Lagunas de Montebello (see page 103), located in Chiapas near Guatemala, a complex of some 60 lagoons, all in different hues.

A splashing fountain delights the eye and ear in Eduardo Ruiz National Park, Michoacán

NATIONAL PARKS

Mexico has over 50 National Parks, covering mountainous, desert, and jungle terrain. Some in the more central regions have marked paths, picnic areas, campgrounds, and lodges. Several parks lie within the state of México and are easily accessible from the capital. At Lagunas de Zempoala, seven turquoise lakes nestle in forested sierra. The romantic Desierto de los Leones, with its old Carmelite monastery, is set in thick pine and oak woods, while the extensive Ajusco National Park rests on the slopes of an inactive volcano. In Michoacán, the enchanting Eduardo Ruiz National Park fairly sings with cascading streams and bubbling springs amidst lush foliage. The Cupatitzio River rises here, and becomes a powerful 60m-high waterfall.

In the tropical regions of the southeast, parks often encompass a landmark of special note. At Cascadas Agua Azul, south of Palenque (see page 103), you can swim amidst sparkling cascades to the sound of tropical birds, while the multi-hued gorge of the Cañon del Sumidero is the highlight of Tuxtla Gutiérrez National Park (see page 103). Bordering Guatemala, the lakes of Lagunas de Montebello National Park (see page 103) are set like dozens of varicolored gems in the orchid-laden wilderness.

In the parched lands of the north, Cumbres de Monterrey National Park features the sheer walls and bizarre rock formations of Huasteca Canyon. Northwest of that lies the extraordinary Copper Canyon National Park (see pages 138–9), with a series of deep interconnecting gorges considerably larger and deeper than America's Grand Canyon. At nearby Basaseáchic Falls National Park, the longest single-drop waterfall in North America tumbles through a natural ridge over gigantic cliffs.

Mountain-spined Baja California has the Sierra San Pedro Mártir National Park, set in a vast plateau up in the peninsula's highest range of peaks. Trails and paths traverse meadows, streams, and fragrant forests of pine, fir, and juniper. Remote and relatively inaccessible, the park appeals to a rare breed of enterprising traveler.

Enquire at your hotel or the local tourist office for information on how to reach these areas. Some of the parks are not easily accessible and can only be reached by car.

VOLCANOES

The snow-capped volcanoes that rise in the southern extreme of the central highlands are among Mexico's most outstanding features. Most famous are the pair known as Popocatépetl (Smoking Mountain) and Iztaccíhuatl (White Lady). The taller Popocatépetl, according to legend, represents an Aztec warrior holding an eternal torch over his beloved Iztaccíhuatl, the princess who died of grief before he could return victorious from battle to claim her hand. On his return, he built two mountains, laid her body on one, and stood holding her funeral torch on the other. Different sections of Iztaccíhuatl are named after parts of her body

Farther east lies the gentler-sloped La Malinche volcano, named after the famous Indian woman who was crucial in Cortés's conquest of Mexico, while in the coastal state of Veracruz rises Pico de Orizaba, Mexico's highest volcano at 5,700m. On the route from Mexico City through Puebla and Orizaba down to Veracruz, there are places where you can see all four peaks.

To the west lie the Nevado de Toluca, with two crater lakes, and the twin Volcán Nevado de Colima and Volcán de Fuego de Colima (Mexico's most active volcano). A newcomer in Michoacán is the Paricutín volcano, which erupted in a cornfield in 1943 without warning and rose rapidly, engulfing two nearby villages in lava. Activity stopped in 1952.

The crater of the Nevado de Toluca volcano

The Copper Canyon Railway Journey

Those with a keen sense of adventure will enjoy a ride through the Barranca del Cobre, or Copper Canyon, in northwestern Mexico. As the Chihuahua Pacífico train travels between Los Mochis and Chihuahua through magnificent scenery, stopovers let you explore the rugged gorges inhabited by the Tarahumara Indians, who still live in caves, and many other areas of interest.

The line was completed in 1961, its railbed having been blasted from the side of the mountain for hundreds of kilometers, with 39 bridges and 86 tunnels. A first-class train runs once daily in each direction between Los Mochis and Chihuahua, meeting midway at Divisadero. It is best to start from Los Mochis, to be sure of passing through the most scenic part of the journey in daylight. Along the journey, the train makes a number of stops, when shunting makes way for freight trains, locals get on and off, and vendors board to sell refreshments and handicrafts. Total

The Basaseáchic waterfall drops from the sheer cliff face into a churning turquoise pool

THE TARAHUMARA AND THE MENNONITES

The Copper Canyon area is the homeland of the Tarahumara Indians, a shy and gentle people who live by farming and selling their handicrafts. Known for their long-distance running, some still live in caves and maintain their old lifestyles, although changes are evident.

The Mennonites, who settled around Cuauhtémoc in the early 1920s, are also farmers, producing apples, cheese, and cured meats. They, too, maintain their own lifestyle and schooling, where only their ancestral German is taught. Distinguishable by their pale complexions, the men wear blue dungarees, while the women sport wide-brimmed hats, long drab skirts, and white stockings in the style of the 1830s.

journey time is about 14 hours – if there are no delays – but do allow time to explore the special attractions at stopovers like Divisadero, Creel, and Cuauhtémoc.

The section between Los Mochis and Divisadero offers great vistas of jagged peaks, deep gorges, and pine forests as the train makes its gradual ascent to the

At Divisadero, where the journey breaks for a short while, the Tarahumara sell their dolls

Copper Canyon. At Divisadero, a short walk takes you to the rim of the canyon, where the view into the mouths of three major canyons is a highlight of the journey. With an overnight stop, you can visit some of the Tarahumara caves and other nearby places of interest.

Farther along the line is the old lumber town of Creel. It makes a good base for excursions through awesome landscapes down into the depths of the canyons, to the old mining areas of La Bufa and Batopilas. This is Tarahumara country, and you are likely to encounter them on your travels. Some of the caves they dwell in around Creel can also be visited. Another worthwhile trip is to the Basaseáchic Waterfall.

After Creel, the journey continues through an area of flat farmlands, grazing cattle and fruit orchards. The next stop, Cuauhtémoc, is worth another stop-over to take a look at the Mennonite colony that lives in the surrounding area. You can visit a bookshop, school, cheese factory, and perhaps a private home on an organized tour.

The train arrives at its final destination in the evening. An overnight stay in Chihuahua will give you time to explore the town (see pages 116–17).

Trips on the Copper Canyon Railway can be arranged through:
Los Mochis: Balderrama Hotels and Tours, Hotel Santa Anita. Tel: 5–39–60 or 5–74–08.
Chihuahua: Turismo al Mar, Reforma 400. Tel: 16–92–32 or 16–59–50. For more information write to Ferrocarilles Naciónales de México, Region Norte, Calles Méndéz y 24, Apartido Portal 46, Chihuahua. Tel: 15–77–56 or 12–22–84.

SANCTUARIES AND NATURE RESERVES

In recent years, Mexico has become ever more aware of the need to protect its wildlife and natural resources. As a result, a growing number of wildlife sanctuaries and biosphere reserves are being established. Ecotourism is now actively promoted, with a view to preserving nature and learning about indigenous cultures, while helping provide local people with a means of livelihood.

Bird watching

The Yucatecan coast is a paradise for bird watchers, being home to countless bird species. The big attraction is the large colonies of pink flamingos at Río Lagartos National Park and the Celestún Wildlife Refuge (see picture below). Río Lagartos, 45km east of Mérida, is a sanctuary for resident flamingos, in addition to herons, pelicans, and numerous other species. The flamingos arrive here in April and lay their eggs in June. In September,

they leave for other estuaries, including Celestún, which is on the Gulf of Mexico coast west of Mérida. Celestún is a major winter migration site for pelicans and cormorants, herons, egrets, and many other birds. In each case, boatmen are ready to take you out on the water to see the flamingos for a negotiable price. Contoy Island, a wildlife preserve inhabited by 60 or so bird species, can be reached on a day trip from Cancún or Isla Mujeres. Enquire at your hotel for information on excursions.

Biosphere reserves

South of Tulum, in Quintana Roo, is the Sian Ka'an Biosphere Reserve, a large area of tropical rain forests, wetlands, and marine habitats shared between 1,000 human residents (mainly Maya) and hundreds of species of plants and animals, some of them endangered. Coastal lagoons and mangrove swamps provide nesting sites for colonies of water birds. Every May sees the arrival of turtles, which lay their eggs on one of

Sleek deer and stealthy jaguar, prey and predator: both are protected in sanctuaries

the last undeveloped stretches of coast in North America. (All-day hikes, which include a three-hour boat trip, can be arranged in Cancún through Amigos de Sian Ka'an, tel: 84–95–83/87–30–80.)

Calakmul is the largest of these reserves, extending from central Campeche down to the Guatemalan border, where it links up with the Maya Biosphere Reserve. Rare orchids, howler monkeys, jaguars, ocelots, and tapirs are some of the species found in its dense, ancient rain forests. Centered around the Mayan ruins of Bonampak, in Chiapas, is the recently established Montes Azules Reserve. This reserve is not easily accessible. Excursions can be arranged from Palenque.

Recently, a biosphere reserve has been set up in the northern Gulf of California. Stretching from the mouth of the Colorado River down to Puerto Peñasco, it protects the area's rich marine ecology and restricts fishing.

Monarch Butterfly Sanctuary

Each year towards the end of October, a region in the highlands of Michoacán suddenly comes alive with the fluttering of black and orange wings. Millions of monarch butterflies, from the northern United States and southern Canada, settle down for the winter in three main areas – Zitácuaro, Ocampo, and Angangueo, located between Toluca and Morelia. (It was only 20 years ago that their place of migration was discovered.) They remain there for the winter, then around the middle of April they return north, hundreds of millions of them.

They are part of an important balance in nature, contributing vitally to pollination, with the result that Michoacán is one of the richest states in Mexico in terms of flowers, fruit, and plant life. The best time to see the monarchs is February or March. Several companies organise tours to the El Rosario sanctuary near Angangueo. Admission is charged.

Baja California

One of Mexico's largest wildlife preserves is for the protection of gray whales (see pages 126–7). It covers several bays and lagoons near Guerrero Negro, halfway down the peninsula's Pacific coast. Whale-watching tours are becoming increasingly popular. Arrangements can be made from Guerrero Negro.

SPA RESORTS

Mexico has numerous thermal springs, the majority in the central highlands. The Aztecs recognized their healing powers, and Emperor Moctezuma is known to have visited the spas at El Penon (close to the capital), Ixtapan de la Sal, and Oaxtepec, among others.

Pleasant spa resorts have grown up around some of these, offering attractive accommodations, thermal baths, and health treatments in soothing surroundings. Swimming, riding, and other recreational activities are often nearby. The environs of Mexico City boast a number of fine establishments, where midweek visits will avoid the crowds.

The quiet, whitewashed resort of Ixtapan de la Sal, about 90km southwest of Mexico City, has several hotels set amidst fresh green lawns and fountains. Apart from the municipal spa, there is the privately run Parque Los Trece Lagos, with Roman-style thermal baths and sulphurous pools for rheumatic

Mineral water baths and mud facial at Ixtapan de la Sal, within reach of the capital

ailments. Golf, tennis, and bowling are just some of the other facilities.

An old favorite, with its feel of a bygone era, is San José Purua, located between Toluca and Morelia. This luxurious spa, recently renovated, is set in lush tropical gardens and perched on the rim of a deep gorge, with stunning views of the mountains and a waterfall. A range of sports facilities complement its health-giving waters.

About 140km southeast of Puebla, the charming town of Tehuacán is famous for supplying most of the bottled water drunk throughout Mexico. The place has several hotels, and its thermal springs have been attracting people since pre-Hispanic times. In the state of Querétaro, 18km north of San Juan del Río, is the picturesque spa resort of Tequisquiapan. Around its many thermal and radioactive springs are several hotels with swimming pools, and golf and riding are available in the vicinity.

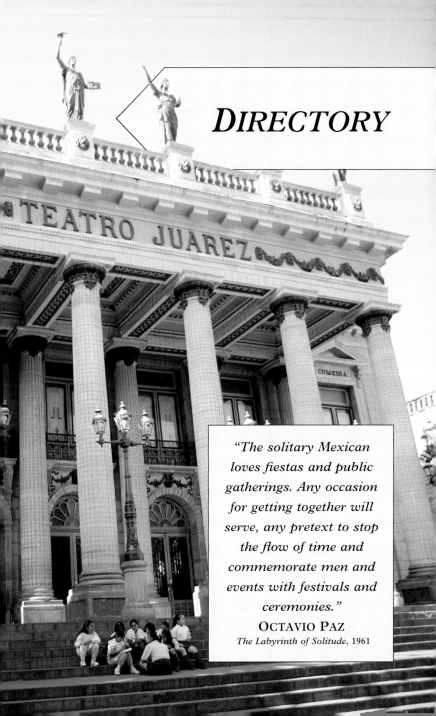

DIRECTORY

"The solitary Mexican loves fiestas and public gatherings. Any occasion for getting together will serve, any pretext to stop the flow of time and commemorate men and events with festivals and ceremonies."

OCTAVIO PAZ
The Labyrinth of Solitude, 1961

Shopping

*F*or sheer variety of colorful products, Mexico is a shopper's delight. Its tradition of handicrafts, or *artesanías*, is very old indeed. Long before the Spanish Conquest, the indigenous peoples were producing pottery, wood carvings, woven goods, and many crafts unique to each region.

The Spaniards introduced new elements of skill, design, and function and helped some Indian communities to develop their existing trades. The result of this marriage of Indian and Spanish talents is a number of top-quality goods that show great flair and imagination. Handicrafts are available in shops and markets throughout Mexico. There are also many centers and shops where you can watch skilled artisans producing their wares.

A Xochimilco souvenir to delight little ones

Points to bear in mind
Most regional handicrafts are also available in Mexico City, and are not necessarily cheaper in their place of origin. It can be more fun, however, to browse around local shops and markets, rather than face the traumas of shopping in a busy capital. In shops, the prices stand as marked, but in markets haggling is expected as part of the game.

Although you can find very attractive goods, quality sometimes falls short of appearance. Always cast a careful eye over merchandise and remember that clothing may not be colorfast or pre-shrunk.

Mexico has lovely semi-precious stones. Don't be persuaded to pay too much for them, and be wary of fake stones. When buying silver, look for the hallmark stamp of .925. Don't confuse this real silver with the cheapish, pretty jewelry called *alpaca*, which is only 25 percent silver. Beware of so-called "genuine" archaeological pieces for sale by the roadside. Good reproductions can be found in reputable shops (besides, it is strictly forbidden to take genuine pieces out of the country).

Organized day trips invariably make a stop or two at handicraft centers, where you are encouraged to spend. You may, of course, find all sorts of attractive items, but bear in mind that the goods may not be of the best quality and may be overpriced.

GOOD BUYS
The following are some of Mexico's best products and regions of production.

Ceramics and pottery
Unglazed earthenware, highly glazed and decorated pottery, ornaments, dishes, etc. Oaxaca, Tlaquepaque, Talavera, Puebla.

Gold filigree-work
Oaxaca, Mérida.

Strut your stuff in a flashy *sombrero*, or just keep cool under a Panama hat

Hammocks
Originally made from cotton, nowadays they are often made from nylon, which is convenient for packing.
Mérida, Veracruz.

Hand-blown glass
Glasses, vases, bowls, and dishes in turquoise, green, or red glass.
Tlaquepaque, Oaxaca, Mexico City.

Lacquerwork
Trays, bowls, boxes, gourds, and items with encrusted decorations.
Pátzcuaro, Olinalá.

Onyx
Similar in appearance to marble, and very popular in Mexico. Chess sets, ashtrays, boxes, bookends, animal figures.
Tecali.

Panama hats
Authentic Panama hats can be rolled up and when unrolled will immediately resume their shape.

Becal, Campeche, Mérida, Michoacán.

Semi-precious stones
Opals, topazes, aquamarines, and amethysts are predominant.
San Juan del Río, Querétaro, Durango.

Silverware and jewelry
Bracelets, earrings, necklaces, rings, and decorative items for the home in beautiful designs, often combining modern and pre-Columbian motifs.
Taxco, Mexico City, Oaxaca, Mérida.

Textiles and traditional garments
Woven brightly colored woolen rugs: Oaxaca, Mitla.
Serapes – a type of woolen blanket, worn poncho-style, usually multi-colored: Saltillo.
Rebozos – brightly colored shawls: San Cristóbal de las Casas.
Guayaberas – embroidered men's shirts with tucks, usually white, but also in other pale colors: Mérida, Mexico City.
Embroidered garments: Oaxaca, Mérida.

Where to Buy

*A*mong the most attractive buys in Mexico are well-made, colorful handicrafts that are unique to the country. Functional or merely decorative, you can pick up any number of delightful souvenirs and gifts at very reasonable prices. It's often a real pleasure to wander around each town, browsing the small shops and markets, but it may be more practical to visit the well setup handicraft stores found in major towns. The following is a brief selection of some specialty shops.

MEXICO CITY
HANDICRAFTS
Bazar Sábado
Colorful market with quality handicrafts, Saturdays only.
Plaza San Jacieto, San Angel.

Casa de los Azulejos
Popular store for a wide range of souvenirs.
Madero 4.

Fonart
State-run chain of stores with attractively presented arts and crafts from all over Mexico.
Londres 136A, Avenida Juárez 89 and Presidente Carranza 115, Coyoacán.

The Green Door
Sells handicrafts, silver jewelry, and high-quality pre-Columbian reproductions.
Cedro 8. Tel: 546–80–05

SILVER, GOLD, AND JEWELRY
Los Castillo
Outstanding quality and designs from an established family firm from Taxco.
Amberes 41. Tel: 511–83–96.

SPECIAL
Aero Boutiques
Large duty-free complex with a wide range of goods.
Mexico City Airport.

OAXACA
BLACK POTTERY
Doña Rosa's Shop
Here you can watch the potters at work.
San Bartolo Coyotepec. 36km south.

HANDICRAFTS
Fonart
Manuel M Bravo 116. Tel: 6–57–64.
La Mano Mágica
Alcala 203. Tel: 6–42–75.

JEWELRY
Oro de Monte Albán
Adolfo C. Gurríon, in front of Santo Domingo Church. Tel: 6–45–28.

SAN MIGUEL DE ALLENDE
ART GALLERIES
Galería San Miguel
Plaza Principal 14. Tel: 2–10–46.
Galería Sergio Bustamante
Known for ceramic, metal, and papier-mâché animal figures.
Mesones.

HANDICRAFTS
Casa Maxwell
Canal 14. Tel: 2–02–47.

TINWARE
La Carretera de Arte
Calle Zacateros 26–A. Tel: 2–17–32.

TAXCO
SILVERWARE AND JEWELRY
Los Castillos
Top-quality craftsmanship and outstanding designs of silverware and jewelry created by the local Castillo brothers.
Plazuela Bernal, Taxco el Viejo. Tel: 2–34–71.

There are hundreds of shops in Taxco filled with attractive silverware, ceramics, and handicrafts. The choice is yours!

TLAQUEPAQUE
CERAMICS
Cerámica Guadalajara
Good selection of ceramics and tiles.
Juárez 347.

Puente Viejo
Known for ceramics and tinware.
Juárez 159.

HAND–BLOWN GLASS
La Rosa de Cristal
Good selection of glassware. You can also watch the craftsmen at their painstaking work.
Calle Independencia 232. Tel: 639–7180.

Tlaquepaque is one of Mexico's most famous handicraft centers, with an abundance of shops. Your best bet is to go for an unhurried exploration of the main shopping area, a pedestrian zone west of the plaza.

Pottery and other collectibles, little and large, at the Parian market, Tlaquepaque

INDIAN MARKETS

For centuries, since the Aztecs bought and sold at their *tianguis*, Mexico has had a tradition of markets. This practice continues to form an integral part of Mexican life, particularly for the indigenous population. Every town has its weekly or daily market, and old Indian markets in the smaller villages are ideal places at which to observe local ways.

Everywhere you look colors are a j[...] to behold

Market day, always exciting, transforms a small place overnight into a sociable scene of bargain and banter. Indian women with long black plaits and numerous children mind their stalls, which are crammed with exotic fruits, fiery chilies, vivid flowers, rainbow-colored rugs, pots, and all manner of fascinating products. Local medicine men call out to advertise strange potions and remedies for ailments. Haggling is standard practice.

Toluca's Friday market is perhaps the best known, but is now too huge. More enjoyable are the ones in Oaxaca (Saturday) and the neighboring

villages of Ocotlán (Friday) and Tlacolula
(Sunday).

Deep in the highlands of Chiapas, the
markets have another flavor. Of special interest
are those of San Cristóbal de las Casas and the
Sunday market of nearby San Juan Chamula.
These are particularly fascinating for being the
gathering places of various Indian groups who
come down from their surrounding hill
communities, dressed in traditional costumes
unique to each village and speaking different
languages.

Entertainment

*W*hen it comes to entertainment in Mexico, the simplest forms are often the most satisfying. Just sitting in a bar or restaurant watching the action can be enjoyable. There is always plenty of music about to liven things up, and no shortage of ambience.

Bandstand concerts in town squares provide great entertainment at no cost. Nightclubs provide another sort of fun, at a noticeable cost! For the young and trendy there are discos galore, especially in the coastal resorts. In major cities, there are concerts, opera, and ballet, and spectacular performances of traditional song and dance are not to be missed.

Information on what's going on in Mexico City can be found in a number of publications, including the daily English-language paper *The News,* and weekly *Tiempo Libre* and *Esta Semana.* Often found in hotels are *Donde* and the annual *Travelers Guide to Mexico.*

BARS

Hotel bars are popular evening meeting places for Mexicans. Many have live music, some have additional entertainment. Typically, they are full of animated conversation and joking. Many in coastal resorts feature loud tropical music and dancing. Otherwise, ordinary bars tend to be private or too local.

MEXICO CITY
Campanario Bar
Magnificent view of the Zócalo.
Majestic Hotel, Madero 73. Tel: 521–86–00.
Galería Plaza Bar
Lively lobby bar; variety of music, including jazz.
Hotel Catería Plaza, Hamburgo 195. Tel: 211–00–14.

Jorongo Bar
Mariachis and other bands.
Sheraton María Isabel Hotel, Reforma 325. Tel: 207–39–33.
Lobby Bar
Popular rendezvous spot.
Camino Real Hotel, Mariano Escobedo 700. Tel: 203–21–21.

ACAPULCO
Bar Acapulco Plaza
Acapulco Plaza Hotel, Costera Miguel Alemán 123. Tel: 85–90–50.
Bar Terraza
Hyatt Regency Hotel, Costera Miguel Alemán 1. Tel: 84–53–63.

CANCÚN
Hard Rock Café
Plaza Lagunas, Paseo Kukulcán. Tel: 83–20–24.
Pat O'Brian's
Flamingo Plaza. Tel: 3–15–44.

PUERTO VALLARTA
El Nido Bar (Chez Elena)
Guitar music and sunset views.
Matamoros 520. Tel: 2–01–61.
Friday López
Fiesta Americana Hotel, Km 2.5 Airport Road. Tel: 4–20–10.

CABARET

Nightclubs with a floor show are getting far and few between these days, having given way to discos and other forms of entertainment.

MEXICO CITY
Barbarella
Nightclub featuring top entertainers.
Hotel Fiesta Americana, Reforma 80. Tel: 705–15–15.
El Patio
Old-time nightclub with occasional star performers.
Atenas 9. Tel: 566–17–43.
El Señorial
Floor show catering mainly to Mexicans.
Hamburgo 188. Tel: 511–97–70.
Maquiavelo
Lively, regular floor shows.
Krystal Hotel, Liverpool 155. Tel: 211–00–92.
Prestige
San Jerónimo 190. Tel: 616–20–20.

CINEMA
Mexicans are avid film-goers, and there are plenty of movie houses in Mexico City to choose from. Larger towns in other parts of the country usually have at least one cinema. Most films are dubbed into Spanish; the few exceptions have subtitles.

MEXICO CITY
Cinética Nacional
Specializes in Mexican and international cultural films.
Avenida México-Coyoacán 389. Tel: 688–32–72.

Classic films are occasionally presented at the Anglo-Mexican Cultural Institute, Antonio Caso 127, and the American Cultural Institute, Hamburgo 115.

CLASSICAL MUSIC, BALLET, AND OPERA
Mexico City and major centers have some fine venues for concerts, opera, and ballet.

MEXICO CITY
Nezahualcoyotl Hall
Striking modern architecture. Classical music.
Insurgentes Sur 3000. Tel: 655–65–11.
Ollin Yolitzli
One of Mexico's finest concert halls.
Periférico Sur 1541. Tel: 606–75–73.
Palacio de Bellas Artes
Top venue for classical music, opera, and ballet.
Avenida Juárez and Eje Central Lázaro Cárdenas. Tel: 709–31–11.

GUADALAJARA
Teatro Degollado
Home of the Guadalajara symphony orchestra. Concerts and opera.
Plaza de la Liberación. Tel: 613–11–15.

GUANAJUATO
Teatro Juárez
Dance, drama, and concerts.
Calle de Sopeña. Tel: 2–01–83.

Dancing to a different beat: disco in Cabo San Lucas (above), flamenco in Mexico City (right)

DISCO DANCING

The liveliest venues are to be found at the beach resorts, where the jetset dance the night away to deafening noise levels. Trends change with unseemly rapidity – this year's hot spot may well be next season's history!

MEXICO CITY
Cero Cero
Camino Real Hotel, Mariano Escobedo 700. Tel: 203–21–21.
Disco Club 84
Stouffer Presidente Hotel, Campos Eliseos 218. Tel: 327–77–00.
Dynasty
Niko Mexico Hotel, Campos Eliseos 204. Tel: 280–11–11.

ACAPULCO
Baby 'O
Ground-breaking nightspot.
Costera Miguel Alemán and Horacio Nelson. Tel: 84–74–74.
Extravaganzza
Carretera Escénica. Tel: 84–71–64.
Fantasy
Carretera Escénica (next to Las Brisas). Tel: 84–67–27.

CANCÚN
Dady 'O
Boulevard Kukulcán, Km 9.5. Tel: 83–33–33.
La Boom
Boulevard Kukulcán, Km 3.5. Tel: 83–11–52.

IXTAPA
Carlos 'n Charlie's
Next to Hotel Posada Real. Tel: 3–00–85.
Christine
Hotel Krystal, Blvd. Ixtapa. Tel: 3–04–56.

PUERTO VALLARTA
Cactus Club
Ignacio Vallarta 399. Tel: 2–60–37.
Christine
Hotel Krystal, Avenida de las Garzas. Tel: 4–02–02.

LOCAL ENTERTAINMENT

In most towns and villages, life revolves around the main square, the zócalo. A most enjoyable hour or two can be spent sitting in a pleasant bar under the surrounding arcades and just watching life go by. Sundays and feast days are particularly lively, when Mexican families are out *en masse*, enjoying the band concerts, local dancing, and other goings-on. The charming custom of serenading is still alive and well. Much serenading is done by the strolling musicians of Guanajuato, known as *estudiantinas*, who cut a dashing figure in their traditional costumes.

TRADITIONAL DANCE AND MUSIC

Mexico's great folk tradition manifests itself in colorful shows of regional songs and dance. An opportunity to see the superb Mexican National Ballet Folklórico should not be missed. Numerous hotels and restaurants in the main centers, in addition to special venues, regularly present highly entertaining Mexican *Fiestas*.

MEXICO CITY
Auditorio Nacional
Reforma and Campo Morte. Tel: 280–92–34.
Focolare Restaurant
Hamburgo 87. Tel: 511–26–79.
Palacio de Bellas Artes
Dazzling presentation of regional songs and dances by the world-famous Ballet Folklórico de México. Wednesday evenings and Sunday mornings.
Avenida Juárez and Eje Central Lázaro Cárdenas. Tel: 512–36–33.
Plaza Garibaldi
Famous square where great numbers of *mariachi* bands congregate.
Plaza Santa Cecilia
Off Garibaldi Square. Tel: 526–24–55.

ACAPULCO
Centro Internacional (Convention Center)
Plaza Mexicana. Tel: 84–70–50.
Marbella Plaza
Costera Miguel Alemán. No telephone.

CANCÚN
Cancún Convention Center
Paseo Kulkulcán Km 9. Tel: 83–01–99.
Hotel Continental Villas Plaza
Paseo Kulkulcán Km 11. Tel: 83–10–95.

GUADALAJARA
Plaza de los Mariachis
Home ground of the *mariachis*, who entertain for money.
Teatro Degollado
Sunday morning performances of the Grupo Folklórico from the University.
Plaza de la Liberación. Tel: 613–11–15.

PUERTO VALLARTA
Camino Real Hotel
Playa Las Estacas. Tel: 3–01–23.
Hotel Krystal Vallarta
Avenida de las Palmas. Tel: 2–14–59.
Hotel Westin Regina
Paseo de la Marina Sur 205. Tel: 1–11–00
La Iguana
Cárdenas 311 (between Constitución and Insurgentes). Tel: 2–01–05.

Fiestas and Fairs

*E*very town and village in Mexico has at least one annual *fiesta*, in addition to nationally celebrated *fiestas* and public holidays, so it's quite possible you will run across one in the course of your travels. Should you wish to see a particular one, check details beforehand, as the date could suddenly change. The following is a selection of some of the best Mexico has to offer.

Mardi Gras (Carnival Week)
Late February/early March. Starts just before Ash Wednesday. Lively celebrations, parades with decorated floats, music, dancing, fireworks. Most colorful in Veracruz and Mazatlán.

Folk dancers at a festival in Baja California

Semana Santa (Holy Week)
From Palm Sunday to Easter Sunday. Celebrated throughout the country. Impressive Passion Play in Ixtapalapa, just outside Mexico City. Beautiful candlelit processions in Taxco.

Feria de San Marcos (St. Mark's Fair)
Around 25 April to 5 May. Lively fair with bullfights, cockfights, *charreadas*, *mariachis*, dancing.

Corpus Christi
May or June. National *fiesta*. Of special interest is the old Totonac ceremony of the *Voladores* (Flying Men) of Papantla, which is given in their home town of Papantla, Veracruz.

Día de San Antonio (St. Anthony's Day)
13 June. Celebrated all over the country. Entertaining in San Miguel de Allende, where Los Locos (The Crazy Ones) parade through town in masks and strange costumes.

La Guelaguetza
Latter part of July. Regional Indian dances with colorful costumes and headdresses, performed on the Cerro del Fortín in Oaxaca. Old tradition going back to the Zapotecs.

Día de la Independencia (Independence Day)
15–16 September. Mexico's most important annual date, commemorating the outbreak of the War of Independence against Spain. Grand celebrations in Mexico City. Highlight is the *Grito,* given by the President from the National Palace on the 15th. The following day is marked by a military parade, including elegant *charros* (Mexican cowboys) on horseback.

Festival Internacional Cervantino (International Cervantes Festival)
October. This cultural festival, named

for the author of *Don Quixote*, has become a big international event in Guanajuato. Over a two-week period there are concerts, plays, opera performances, and other cultural events, with participants from many nations.

Fiestas de Octubre (October Festival)

Guadalajara sees a month of continuous celebrations, with concerts, art exhibitions, and numerous sporting and cultural events, crowned by glorious firework displays.

Día de los Muertos (Day of the Dead)

1–2 November. Celebrated nationally, but quite unique on the tiny island of Janitzio, in Lake Pátzcuaro. At midnight, the villagers go to the cemetery with torches and candles, bearing flowers and food offerings for their departed ones. The whole island comes alive with thousands of flickering lights as the natives take part in the all-night wake.

Día de Nuestra Señora de Guadalupe (Festival of Our Lady of Guadalupe)

12 December. Commemoration Day of the Patroness of Mexico. Endless processions of pilgrims arrive in Mexico City from all over to pay homage at the Virgin's shrine, the Basilica of Guadalupe, one of the most revered in the country. Regional dancers in resplendent costumes perform native dances in front of the Basilica.

In Champotón, Campeche, a religious procession follows behind a banner portraying Our Lady of Guadalupe

FIESTAS

*F*iesta – the very word conjures up images of music, laughter, dancing, feasting – and in Mexico *fiestas* are a way of life, an institution that verges on the sacred, an opportunity to set problems to one side and rejoice in the sheer vitality of it all. In all seasons, for all reasons, Mexicans sprinkle these celebrations through the calendar like confetti. Whether marking a religious occasion or a secular one, Mexicans do it with an abundance of flair and merriment.

Some *fiestas* go back to pagan times, relating to aspects of nature such as fertility or the harvest; these still contain ancient Indian customs and beliefs. Many others entered the picture with Christianity, and have a strongly Spanish flavor. Most combine elements of both, and any apparent contradictions between the two cultures are overlooked in the general *bonhomie* arising out of parading, dressing up, music-making – and not a little drinking, often rounded off for good measure with fireworks.

Each region cherishes its own style of celebrating, and this is proudly displayed in traditional music and dance. Jalisco's infectious *mariachi* rhythms, Veracruz's merry *sones*, the Yucatán's romantic *trovas* and graceful dancers, the Western-style sound of *norteño* music – all present a delightfully different facet of the Mexican character.

Some of the dances survived the culture shock of the Conquest, and continue to impress today's visitors as

Onlookers cheer the bizarre-looking animal skin dancers at Guadalupe

they undoubtedly did the first Spaniards. See, if you can, the *Venado* (stag dance) from Sonora in the north; the dance of the *Viejitos* (old men) from Michoacán; the *Panachos* (feather dance) from Oaxaca; or the *Quetzales*, with striking wheel-like headdresses, from Cuetsalán, Puebla. Whatever form it takes, each artistic expression personifies its locality while contributing uniquely to Mexico's complex heritage.

Uninhibited fun for all in San Miguel de Allende on the feast of St. Anthony

Children

*M*exicans are well known for their love of children, and you can be sure yours will be welcome and shown every consideration. Your best bet is to select a coastal resort with a good beach and pool, then spend your time in that area. Apart from the swimming, there are often many additional attractions, such as horse or donkey rides along the beach, boat trips around the bay, and other children to play with.

Touring around with young children is not ideal. Heat, upset stomachs, delays, and all sorts of problems can arise, and many major sights are geared to adult interests. However, there is plenty in Mexico that will appeal to children: lakeside resorts, *hacienda*-type hotels in beautiful gardens, colorful markets, and lively *fiestas* where people of all ages catch the *camaraderie*. The zoological gardens dotted about the country are also well worth visiting if you're in the vicinity. The following are some special attractions that children might enjoy.

MEXICO CITY AND SURROUNDINGS
Nuevo Reina Aventura

Theme park including model villages, Children's World, performing dolphins. *Carretera Picacho a Ajusco, south of the city. Tel: 654-54-34. Open: Friday to*

Sunday 10am–6.30pm, Daily July,
August. Admission charge.

Zoológico de Chapultepec
Children's zoo, pony riding, miniature
railway, boating on the lake. Amusement
park and roller coaster.
*Section 1 of Chapultepec Park. Tel:
553–62–29. Open Tuesday to Sunday
10am–5pm. Free*

ACAPULCO
CICI
See page 79.

Papagayo Park
See page 79.

GUADALAJARA
Parque Agua Azul
Large park with aviary, butterfly
sanctuary, mini train rides for children.
*Calzada Independencia Sur and Avenida
de Campesino. Tel: 619–13–28. Open:
Tuesday to Sunday 10am–6pm. Admission
charge.*

**Parque Natural Huentitán Zoológico
Guadalajara**
Zoological gardens with animals in
natural setting. Large aviary. Tours by
mini trains. Adjoining is the Selva Mágica
(Magic Jungle) Amusement Park.
*Paseo del Zoológico 600. Tel: 674–10–34.
Open: Tuesday to Sunday 10am–6pm.
Admission charge.*

Planetario Severo Díaz Galino
Planetarium with hands-on exhibits.
*Avenida Ricardo Flores Magón 599. Tel:
674–41–06. Open: Tuesday to Sunday
10am–7pm. Admission charge.*

Language is no barrier between children at the
wide beach of Playa Azul in Michoacán

Polychrome parrot at Tuxtla Zoomat

PUEBLA
Zoológico Africam
Safari-type zoo with large selection of
animals.
*21km southeast of Puebla. Tel: 35–87–00.
Open: daily 10am–5pm. Admission charge.*

TOLUCA
Zacango Zoo
Animals are free to wander about in
lovely grounds, formerly part of an old
ranch. Special attraction is a spacious
walk-through aviary.
*Off highway between Toluca and Ixtapan
de la Sal. Tel: 17–63–15. Open: Tuesday to
Sunday 10am–6pm. Admission charge.*

TUXTLA GUTIÉRREZ
Zoomat
One of the best zoological gardens in
Mexico. All species are from Chiapas
state and include jaguars, monkeys, a
large tapir, brilliantly colored tropical
birds, and an impressive reptile house.
Magnificent setting in a natural jungle
habitat, where the animals can roam
around spacious enclosures.
*Southeast of town, just off Libramiento
Sur. Open: Tuesday to Sunday 8:30am–
5:30pm. Admission free.*

Sports

*F*or those who wish to be active, there is plenty of choice. In major towns, there is golf, tennis, and horseback riding, while beach resorts have facilities for all your favorite water sports (the Caribbean is a veritable diver's paradise). *Charreadas*, bullfights, and jai alai matches have that special Mexican flavor.

SPECTATOR SPORTS
For information, tickets, or guided tours, ask at your hotel, local tourist office, or a travel agency.

Bullfights
Bullfighting is practically a national institution in Mexico, and most towns have a bullring. The main season is December through March, when the professionals perform in Mexico City's Plaza México, Calle A Rodín s/n (tel: 563–39–59). Bullfights, or *corridas*, are held on Sundays, and normally start promptly at 4pm.

The impressive entrance to Tijuana's bullring

Charreadas
Charreadas are Mexican-style rodeos, with displays of horsemanship by *charros* in dashing outfits. Girl riders, singers and *mariachi* bands combine to make this a very colorful show. In Mexico City, performances are held most Sunday mornings at the Lienzo del Charro (take the Picacho turning off the Periférico west of San Ángel) or the Rancho del Charro (just off Avenida Constituyentes, Chapultepec Park).

Football (Soccer)
As in most of Latin America, the Mexicans are crazy about *futbol*. In Mexico City, matches are held in the

Aztec Stadium, SA–Tlalpan 3465 (tel: 677–71–98) and the Olympic Stadium, University City (tel: 550–06–80).

Horse racing
Mexico City's Hipódromo de las Américas, off Avenida Manuel Ávila Camacho (tel: 557–41–00), offers thoroughbred horse racing daily, except for Mondays and Wednesdays. Small admission fee.

Jai alai
This fast and skillful game from the Basque country is a very popular spectator sport in Mexico, with a tremendous buildup of excitement as continuous betting goes on. Matches are held in the capital at the Frontón México, Plaza de la República (tel: 546–32–40) Tuesday to Saturday evenings at 7pm and Sunday from 5pm.

PARTICIPANT SPORTS
Hotels and local tourist offices can provide information on a variety of sports.

Golf
Magnificent 18-hole golf courses are features at all the major tourist centers, where they are usually attached to hotels. Some resorts boast several courses, with the number of new ones growing each season. In and around major towns are elegant country golf clubs, where visitors can play as the guest of a member or may be admitted on weekdays for a daily fee. *For information contact Federación Mexicana de Golf, Avenida Lomas de Sotelo III, México DF 11200 (tel: 395–86–42).*

Hunting
Many regions of Mexico offer hunting, for both large game (including the desert mule deer, bighorn sheep, antelope, and peccary) and small (squirrels, coyotes, armadillos, etc). There is also wing-shooting for ducks, geese, quail, and doves. Always apply well in advance to book your hunt with a registered outfitter. It is best to rent equipment in Mexico, and obtain a local hunting permit, also arranged through the outfitter. *For information and the hunting season calendar write to the Secretaría de Agricultura y Recursos Hidraulicos, Dirección General de Flora y Fauna Silvestre, Nuevo León 210, Piso 19, Col Hipodromo Condesa, 06100 México DF (tel: 574–54–89 and 584–58–27). Details on registered outfitters can be obtained from Claudia Ramsower, Mexico City (tel: 741–55–18).*

Horseback riding
Opportunities are endless, from ranch hotels and beach rides at resorts to organized expeditions in such exotic regions as the Copper Canyon or the highlands of Chiapas. Many rides take you through small villages and communities, giving you a rare glimpse of local life. San Miguel de Allende is known for its equestrian school, which caters to the serious rider seeking an intensive training course.

Tennis
Tennis courts are attached to hotels in all popular resorts. In addition, Mexico City, Guadalajara, and major towns have private tennis clubs where visitors can be invited to play by a member. In Puerto Vallarta, enthusiasts will enjoy the John Newcombe Tennis Center next to the Plaza Vallarta Hotel. *For information contact the Federación Mexicana de Tenis, Miguel Angel de Quevado 953, Coyoacán, México DF 04330 (tel: 689–97–33).*

Water Sports

Boating and sailing

Mexico's coastal resorts, lakes, and reservoirs offer ample opportunities for boating and sailing. All sorts of seagoing vessels can be rented in major resorts, ranging from canoes, catamarans, and kayaks to sailboats and large yachts.

Within range of Mexico City, the lakes of Tequesquitengo, Zempoala, Avandaro, and Valsequillo Dam have boats for rent. Weather conditions are usually favorable during the winter months. Regattas are held in some resorts, including Acapulco, Cozumel, Ensenada, Manzanillo, and Mazatlán.

Deep-sea fishing

Mexico's long Pacific coastline is renowned for its excellent deep-sea fishing, considered by many to rank with the best in the world. North Americans have been traveling down for years to fish in the Gulf of California. Main centers for fishing are Guaymas, Mazatlán, Manzanillo, Ensenada, and Los Cabos, where charter boats and equipment are available. You can get a fishing license through the local Fisheries Department office, or through the captain of your chartered boat. Catch includes marlin, sailfish, swordfish, tuna, and shark. *For information on fishing and permits contact the Secretaría de Pesca, Alvaro Obregón 269, 06700 México DF (tel: 211–00–63).*

Freshwater fishing

In recent years, Mexico has become known for its excellent black bass fishing. Two of the best spots for this are the Vicente Guerrero Dam in Tamaulipas, and the Comedero Dam in Sinaloa. In the central area, fishing is possible in the lakes of Zempoala, Valle de Bravo, Pátzcuaro, Chapala, and many other lakes and reservoirs. Fishing tackle is for rent at some centers.

Parasailing

Parasailing continues as a popular pastime in the top resorts. Dangling beneath a parachute at the mercy of a speedboat far below you may not appeal to everybody. However, for the sensation and the views, it's worth trying – at least once!

LOS DORADOS
SPORTFISHING
Office Hotel Plaza las Glorias   Phone 3-16-30

Sailing and sport-fishing at Cabo San Lucas, snorkeling with scaly friends at Xel-Há: just a few of the aquatic experiences in Mexico

Scuba diving and snorkeling

Mexico has developed into an idyllic destination for underwater enthusiasts. Many areas along its beautiful coastline offer excellent scuba diving and snorkeling. Conditions are ideal in the Caribbean, where crystal-clear waters and coral reefs are the habitat of countless varieties of tropical fish. In the Yucatán Peninsula, many lagoons and *cenotes* (sinkholes) provide superb diving experiences. Outstanding are the interlocking lagoons of Xel-Há and the underground rivers and caves of Xcaret. At Akumal Bay, famous for scuba diving, there is expert instruction. Cozumel is renowned for its Palancar reef and the underwater caves of the Chancanab lagoon. El Garrafón in Isla Mujeres has a fascinating underwater coral garden.

There is also good diving and snorkeling on the Pacific coast. Among some excellent spots is the area near El Arco and also tranquil Santa Maria Bay in Cabo San Lucas, Baja California.

Surfing

Pacific waves can reach tremendous heights, which makes for world-class surfing beaches. The sport has rapidly gained in popularity, and enthusiasts are discovering new areas. Some of the best beaches are around Puerto Escondido, Huatulco, Mazatlán, and in Baja California. The island of Todos Santos, off Ensenada, is considered one of the top spots, only to be attempted by experts. Surfboards can be rented at most major resorts.

Windsurfing

Windsurfing has caught on in a big way and is available in most resorts, with lessons if needed (just inquire on the beach). The sport is particularly popular in Cancún, which has ideal conditions and holds international competitions. The International Windsurfing Sailing School (tel: 84–20–23) rents out equipment and gives instruction. The National Windsurfing Tournament is held annually in Cancún in July.

Food and Drink

*M*exican cuisine is a combination of traditional Indian dishes and later influences from Spanish, French, and other European cuisines. Its distinctive character can only be properly experienced in Mexico itself. Forget the myth that all Mexican food is hot and spicy. While hot chilies are used in certain recipes, they do not dominate the cuisine. A word to the wise, however: be cautious in trying the small bowls of sauce (salsa) that accompany many dishes. They may look similar, but can range from the bland to blistering!

The basics

Maize and beans were cultivated in Mexico by early settlers. With their nutritional value, they continue to form the staple diet of many Mexicans today. No self-respecting Mexican meal is complete without its *tortillas*. Made from maize flour and formed into pancakes, they are eaten as a kind of bread with the meal. *Tortillas* form the basis of numerous dishes. Stuffed, they become *tacos*. Topped with a sauce and baked, they are called *enchiladas*. *Quesadillas, tostadas, burritos,* and *chilaquiles* are only some of the variations of *tortilla*-based dishes. Served with a portion of *refritos* (refried beans) and avocado-based *guacamole*, these form the basics of Mexican food.

Regional cooking

Each region has its own style and specialties, some of which can be sampled in restaurants all over Mexico. Oaxaca and Puebla (of *mole poblano* fame) are noted for good traditional cooking. The Yucatán offers tasty pork, fiery chilies, and delicately flavored dishes steamed in banana leaves. The best beef comes mostly from the cattle ranches of Chihuahua, while Monterrey is known for *cabrito* (roast kid).

Coastal resorts offer a great variety of seafood, and an abundance of charming open-air restaurants in which to sample it. A popular dish is *ceviche*, fish marinated in lime juice. Veracruz and Campeche, on the Gulf of Mexico, are renowned for the quality of their fish.

Eating out

Eating out in Mexico is fun. Mexico City and major towns offer a wide selection, ranging from

Dine at the captain's table in Zihuatanejo

the ultra-sophisticated to traditional Mexican establishments. Mexico is notorious for its long luncheons, which can last from 2pm till well past sundown. You can eat as little or as much as you like, without feeling pressured. But watch out for waiters with a mania for whipping everything away – sometimes before you've finished. Many restaurants offer international as well as Mexican dishes, the latter being generally cheaper. The following are likely to be included in a typical menu.

Heavily garnished *guacamole* with *tortilla* chips

When the Spanish *conquistadores* arrived, they discovered delicious and wholesome new foods native to Mexico. Among these were sweetcorn and beans (which the Indians had long cultivated), tomatoes, pumpkins, peanuts, avocados, zucchinis, turkeys, chilies, pineapples, vanilla, spices, and cacao (chocolate was known to be a favorite drink of Aztec Emperor Moctezuma). All these foodstuffs were introduced to Europe, and are now taken for granted as part of its normal diet. Maize has become an important crop worldwide, and beans are valued for their high-quality protein and fiber.

Carne asada a la tampiqueña grilled meat with accompaniments
Ceviche fish marinated in lime juice
Chiles rellenos green peppers stuffed with spicy minced beef or cheese
Huevos rancheros fried eggs with tomato sauce atop *tortillas* spread with refried beans
Mole poblano turkey or chicken with rich sauce
Sopa de tortilla broth with strips of *tortilla*
Tacos de pollo chicken-filled *tortillas*
Tamales steamed corn husks filled with meat.

The choice of desserts tends to be limited. There is flan (crème caramel) or plentiful ice-cream (*helado*).

Just like mama makes them? *Tortillas* coming off a simple assembly line in Mexico City

A fresh start to the day: the breakfast buffet at the Hotel Calinda in Guadalajara

MEXICAN BUFFET BREAKFASTS

Breakfast in a Mexican hotel is in a category of its own. First, there is the ambience (business meetings are regularly conducted over breakfast), then there is the buffet, which is offered by most top-class hotels.

The array of dishes is nothing short of splendid. Apart from the whole range of tropical fruits and juices, there are all sorts of hot dishes with tempting accompaniments. Staff will always explain them to you if you ask, or even if you don't! For something hot to drink, there's the familiar choice of coffee, tea, and chocolate. (Coffee, once poor in quality, has greatly improved in recent years.) Some popular dishes are *huevos revueltos a la mexicana* (scrambled eggs with chopped tomato, onion, and chilli), *huevos rancheros* (fried eggs with a spicy tomato sauce), and *chilaquiles* (*tortillas* in a sauce). You will even have the option of a steak. A hearty Mexican breakfast certainly goes a long way!

FRUITS

The selection of tropical fruits in Mexico is vast. Year round you can enjoy mangoes, pineapples, papayas, guavas, melons, watermelons, *tuna* (cactus fruit), oranges, apples, and – instead of lemons – limes, which give that special Mexican flavor to everything. The breakfast fruit platter is a good way to enjoy them.

DRINKS AND BEVERAGES

Mexico's foremost alcoholic beverage, *tequila*, needs no introduction. This plant-based spirit has become internationally famous, and its Margarita and Tequila Sunrise cocktails are known in bars all over the world. The traditional way to drink *tequila* is to take it straight, with a pinch of salt and suck of a lime. An unusual but delicious concoction is *tequila*, lime juice, and Maggi (a brand-name savory liquid seasoning). Lesser known, but equally potent, is *mezcal* and the low-alcohol *pulque*, also derived like *tequila* from the maguey plant (see pages 168–9).

Rum, another product of Mexico, is used in many cocktails. The famous Cuba Libre (rum, lime, and Coke) and Planter's Punch are popular rum-based drinks. Kahlua is a pleasant coffee-flavor liqueur.

Many varieties of beer are produced in Mexico, mainly in the north and the Yucatán, and they perfectly complement the national cuisine. Whether *clara* (light) or *oscura* (dark), they are customarily served chilled. Some of the most popular brands are Superior, Bohemia, Corona, Dos Equis, and Carta Blanca.

Although a wine producer, Mexico is not a wine-drinking country as such. However, the industry is growing and the quality of the wines has greatly improved in recent years. Wine-growing areas are in Baja California and central Mexico. Calafia wine from Baja California is an acceptable table wine.

The so-called *café americano* tends to be weak, but many places now offer espresso. An alternative is *café de olla* (coffee with cinnamon), served in tiny earthenware cups. Mexicans drink a lot of tea. Try it with lime, as they do.

MARGARITA

3 parts *tequila*
1 part Triple Sec (or Cointreau)
2 parts lime juice
Shake with ice, or mix in a blender and strain into cocktail glasses whose rims have been dipped in lime juice and frosted with salt.

Street vendors sell tempting fruits to fill any gap left between meals, but wash them first

What to be wary of

To avoid stomach problems (called *turista*, Montezuma's Revenge, or the Aztec Two-Step), take sensible precautions. Steer clear of salads except in American-style hotels in major resorts; peel fruit. Be careful of pork in tropical locations. Do not drink tap water. Avoid unpasteurized milk. Resist the temptation of buying food from roadside stalls. See **Health** on page 184.

Mexico imparts a whole new meaning to the term "fruit cocktail"

TEQUILA,

Vast plantations of the agave plant are a familiar sight in Mexico. From the 400 or so existing species, a few are used for the production of three native liquors – *tequila*, *mezcal*, and *pulque* – each of which is made from a different variety.

Tequila and *mezcal* are intoxicants produced by a process of fermentation, followed by distillation, while *pulque* is made by fermentation alone, and is low in alcohol content.

Tequila is, in fact, a high-quality variant of *mezcal*. It is produced only from the blue maguey, or the *agave tequilana*, which grows around the towns of Tequila and Tepatitlán, near Guadalajara, Jalisco. A visit to one of the many distilleries in the area might help unravel the mysteries of the legendary liquor. After your *tequila* tasting, all will become clear!

Basically, the center of the maguey

is cut out, roasted, and mashed. This is then placed into fermenting barrels to which yeast is added. The fermented mash is then distilled twice. Colorless *tequila* is bottled directly from the barrel, while older *tequila* acquires a golden color. *Conmemorativo* is a

MEZCAL, AND *PULQUE*

A bottle, lime, salt: all you need to savor *tequila*.
Agaves: spiky for *tequila*, round for *mezcal*.
Taste, then buy in the *mezcal* factory

tequila, which has acquired international status, *mezcal* is mainly for local consumption and is exported on a limited basis. It is quite usual to find a worm (*gusano de maguey*) in the bottom of the bottle. If this does not appeal, stick to *tequila*.

Pulque is an ancient type of nectar dating back to long before the arrival of the Spaniards. It is served in *pulquerías*, where strangers are not too welcome and women are rarely seen.

top-quality tequila that has aged for seven years or more.

Mezcal-producing areas are located in the southeast, southwest, and northern regions of Mexico. Unlike

Where to Eat

*A*lthough the cost of eating out in Mexico has risen in recent years, the *peso* devaluation in 1995 has evened out prices. In major centers, restaurants in all price caterories can be found, ranging from top-class, international establishments to inexpensive, local eateries.

In the listings below, the **N$** (*nuevo peso*) symbols indicate a typical cost per person, excluding drinks. Service is rarely included, and a tip of 10–15 percent is expected to be added on top.

N$1 N$100 and under
N$2 N$P100–NP150
N$3 N$150–NP200
N$4 N$200 and over

MEXICO CITY
INTERNATIONAL
Bellinghausen N$3
Popular Zona Rosa restaurant with attractive outdoor patio. Busy at lunchtime.
Londres 95, Zona Rosa. Tel: 525–87–38.

Estoril N$4
Elegant restaurant, known for its excellent cuisine, housed in an attractive mansion in the Polanco district. Patronized by the smart set.
Alejandro Dumas 24, Polanco. Tel: 280–98–28.
Hacienda de los Morales N$4
Magnificent setting in 17th-century former *hacienda*.
Vázquez de Mella 525. Tel: 540–32–25.
La Calesa de Londres N$4
Lovely setting in old mansion; known for its top-class cuts of beef.
Londres 102. Tel: 533–66–25.

Locals enjoying a sociable get-together at El Indito restaurant in Taxco

San Angel Inn N$4
Located 45 minutes south of the center, but worth the journey for its setting in a restored 18th-century *hacienda*.
Diego Rivera 50, corner of Altavista and San Angel. Tel: 616–14–02.

EUROPEAN
Chalet Suizo N$2
Cosy atmosphere. Swiss and German specialties including fondue.
Niza 37. Tel: 511–75–29.
Meson del Cid N$3
Attractive setting. Authentic Spanish dishes with special suckling pig ceremony.
Humboldt 61. Tel: 521–19–40.
Piccadilly Pub N$3
Located on the pedestrian street of Zona Rosa. Part open-air, handsome English-style interior. Some English dishes.
Copenhague 23. Tel: 525–22–92.

MEXICAN
Fonda el Refugio N$2
Good reputation for classic dishes (even Mexicans line up to get a table).
Liverpool 166. Tel: 207–27–32.
La Fonda del Recuerdo N$2
Lively, good fun, with rousing Veracruzano music, but becoming commercialized with bus tours.
Bahía de las Palmas 37. Tel: 260–05–45.
Los Girasoles N$2
Good location downtown, with lively ambience. Succulent marrowbone is one of the retsaurant's special delicacies.
Calle de Tacuba, Plaza Manuel Tolsa. Tel: 510–06–30.

SPECIAL
Majestic Hotel N$2
Sunday Mexican buffet lunch. Traditional music, view over the Zócalo.
Madero 73. Tel: 521–86–00.

ACAPULCO
Beto's N$2
Three adjoining beach restaurants.
Costera Miguel Alemán. Tel: 84–04–73.
Casanova N$4
Italian cuisine, spectacular view of Acapulco Bay, a romantic setting for dinner *à deux*.
By entrance to Las Brisas. Tel: 84–68–15.
El Embarcadero N$3
Exotic Polynesian-style restaurant in tropical gardens.
Costera Miguel Alemán, near La Palapa Hotel. Tel: 84–87–87.

CANCÚN
Captain's Cove N$2
Known for its good seafood and grilled steaks.
Nichupté Lagoon, facing the Royal Mayan Hotel. Tel: 85–00–16. Also beach by Casas Maya Hotel. Tel: 83–06–69.

MÉRIDA
Los Almendros N$2
Good Yucatecan cuisine, lively ambience.
Calle 50–A, no. 493. Tel: 28–54–59.

OAXACA
Asador Vasco N$3
Spanish dishes. Attractive position overlooking the zócalo.
Portal de Flores. 10-A, 1st floor. Tel: 4–47–55.

PUERTO VALLARTA
Carlos O'Brian's N$2
Popular with the younger set for its informal ambience and lively evenings.
Paseo Díaz Ordáz 786. Tel: 2–14–44.
Daiquiri Dick's N$2
This old favorite, right on the beach, serves Mexican and Californian dishes.
Olas Altas, Los Muertos Beach. Tel: 2–05–66.

Accommodations

Mexico has accommodations to suit all types of clientele, from the vacationer or budget traveler to the businessman. Ultra-modern, high-rise hotels in coastal resorts contrast with charming colonial-style accommodations in the interior of the country.

Although government ratings were eliminated in 1993, hotels continue to use a rating system as follows: Categoría Especial, or CEsp (special properties with distinctive features); Gran Turismo or GT (establishments with amenities of exceptionally high quality); five-star down to one-star; Categoría Económica (or economy); and Sin Categoría (no category). This rating system should only be used as a guideline, based primarily on amenities offered. A number of hotels also carry an AAA (American Automobile Association) diamond rating, according to AAA inspections.

The following approximate double-room rates are given in local currency, excluding the 10–15 per cent IVA (VAT) and 2 per cent lodging tax now charged in some states. These are subject to change and higher seasonal tariffs in coastal resorts (around mid-December to mid-April). Bear in mind that room rates can be considerably lower when part of a package deal. Some hotels in Mexico City also offer lower weekend rates.

Categoría Especial over N\$1,500
Gran Turismo N\$1,300–1,500
5-star N\$1,000–1,300
4-star N\$900–1,000
3-star N\$600–900
2-star N\$500–600
1-star N\$300–500.

Top deluxe hotels in Mexico usually adhere to the highest worldwide standards of service, while establishments in the medium category can often provide comfort, coupled with a more personal atmosphere. Rooms are generally spacious and attractively decorated. In the upper categories you can expect to find a color TV, mini-bar, private bathroom, all the usual facilities, and sometimes the convenience of your own in-room safety deposit box.

Grandness to match its name: the Hotel Ciudad de Mexico, in the nation's capital

A few tips

Drink purified bottled water, even if the tap water is said to be *potable* (drinkable). Be warned about the high cost of long-distance telephone calls from your hotel room. Avoid an unpleasant surprise by using a payphone, or reverse the charges.

MAJOR HOTEL CHAINS
(representatives in Mexico City)

Aristos Hotels *Tel: 564–84–84.*
Best Western *Tel: 208–89–69.*
Camino Real *Tel: 227–72–00.*
Club/Royal Maeva *Tel: 227–02–44.*
Club Med *Tel: 203–31–94.*
Continental Plaza *Tel: 211–51–11*
Day's Inn *Tel: 514–04–40.*
Diamond Hotels *Tel: 858–22–58.*
Four Seasons *Tel: 230–18–18.*
Holiday Inn *Tel: 627–02–99.*
Hoteles del Prado *Tel: 254–44–00.*

Howard Johnson *Tel: 521–02–02.*
Hyatt International *Tel: 626–78–78.*
Krystal *Tel: 511–87–79.*
Marriott *Tel: 207–10–16.*
Meliá *Tel: 251–22–79.*
Mision Hotels *Tel: 207–13–49.*
Omni Hotels *Tel: 227–04–84.*
Posadas de Mexico (Fiesta Americana) *Tel: 326–69–00.*
Presidente Inter-Continental *Tel: 327–77–77.*
Princess Hotels *Tel: 223–69–00.*
Quality Inn (Calinda) *Tel: 208–67–33.*
Radisson *Tel: 606–42–11.*
Ramada *Tel: 705–39–96.*
Sheraton *Tel: 207–39–33.*
Small Grand Hotels of Mexico *Tel: 223–65–10.*
Westin Hotels *Tel: 227–05–55.*

Hotel Acapulco Princess at Pierre Marques

Character in abundance at the Hotel San Diego in Guanajuato

BUSINESS HOTELS

The businessperson is well catered to in Mexico City and other major destinations such as Acapulco, Cancún, Guadalajara, and Monterrey. The larger hotels have executive suites and facilities for meetings and conventions. They can also offer fax, secretarial, translating, and many other professional services.

The Nikko, Camino Real, and María Isabel Sheraton are among the top business hotels in Mexico City, and can host conventions both large and small, supplying all the necessary equipment. The smaller Clarion Reforma Suites cater specially to the businessperson, claiming to be able to meet virtually any requirements, from technical equipment to multilingual interpreting services and arrangement of private transportation. Most rooms are deluxe suites, some complete with Jacuzzi.

BEACH HOTELS

Magnificent hotels line the shores of Mexico's popular resorts. High-rise buildings are much in evidence, but some resorts such as Cancún feature more adventurous architecture. The majority of hotels are on the beach and are set in tropical gardens, with one or more swimming pools to supplement what nature provides. These are most attractively designed and offer all the comforts of loungers, cocktail service (or even swim-up bars), and blissfully warm water.

Beaches tend to attract the energetic

crowd. Many are constantly in motion, with a host of aquatic sports such as boating, water-skiing, parasailing, scuba diving, snorkeling, and windsurfing.

RESORT COMPLEXES

A number of hotels are in a class of their own, and are virtually resorts in themselves. Two outstanding examples are to be found in Acapulco: the world-famous Las Brisas, with its bungalows, individual swimming pools, and stunning views of Acapulco Bay, and the exciting pyramid-shaped Acapulco Princess. Hotel complexes continue to spring up along Mexico's Pacific and Caribbean coastlines, each with its own individual character. Dotted along the beautiful, wild stretch of coast between Puerto Vallarta and Manzanillo, known as the Costa de Oro (Gold Coast), are a number of contrasting hotels. Among the most attractive are Las Hadas, a spectacular Arabian Nights-type fantasy featured in the film *10* and dreamed up by Bolivian tin king Antenor Patiño; the charming Bel-Air Costa Careyes; Los Angeles Locos (The Crazy Angels); and Las Alamandas, exclusive property of Isabel Goldsmith. Mexico's Caribbean coast between Cancún and Tulúm – the Cancún Corridor – also features many lovely complexes, including the new Puerto Aventuras development.

COLONIAL-STYLE HOTELS

In the interior of the country are a number of picturesque hotels that were *haciendas* (ranch houses) back in colonial times. Set in lovely surroundings, they usually offer swimming, tennis, horseback riding, and other pastimes. Weekends tend to be busy with Mexican families. The Hacienda Vista Hermosa, Hacienda Cocoyoc, Mansión Galindo

and Antigua Hacienda de Galindo, Hacienda Juríca, and Hotel San Miguel Reglas are among the most magnificent.

CONDOMINIUMS AND APARTMENTS

Major coastal resorts such as Acapulco, Puerto Vallarta, and Cancún have large, modern condominiums (condos) for rent. Most are located on the beach and consist of large, self-contained apartments, fully furnished and equipped with all amenities. Prices are medium to expensive. Some are operated by large companies in Mexico, and can be booked through rental agencies in the capital.

YOUTH HOSTELS

Only a handful of youth hostels are to be found, spread over the country. Information can be obtained from the Dirección de Alención a la Juventud, Calzada de Ilalpan 583, Colonia Alamo, Mexico DF. Tel: 519–40–29. Also Coordinación Nacional de Tourismo, Glorieta Metro Insurgentes, Local CC-11, Colonia Juárez, Mexico DF. Tel: 525–25–48.

PRICES (double room per night)
Business hotels: year-round N$1,600–2,200.
Beach hotels: high season – N$500–2,600 (rates are generally reduced by about 30 per cent in the low season – around mid-April to mid-December.)
Resort complexes: high season – N$550–2,400 (see above for low season reductions).
Colonial-style hotels: year-round N$530–1,300.
Youth hostels: on average per person N$80–100.

HACIENDAS

After the Conquest, the Spaniards started to develop agriculture and mining, acquiring ever more land and establishing large estates called *haciendas*. These estates developed in the mining areas of the central highlands and the north, in the cattle regions of the dry central plains, Chiapas and Veracruz, in the sugarcane areas around the humid Gulf of Mexico and Morelos, the *henequen* region of the Yucatán, the coffee- and tobacco-growing areas of Veracruz, and the cotton plantations in Coahuila.

Under the Spanish system of land grants, the owner was the absolute ruler over his Indian workers, who lived on the estate and were beholden to him. For 300 years, there was much growth and prosperity for the Spaniards. Although they lost their rule in 1821, the familiar *hacienda* system remained the same.

Great changes, however, were brought about by the 1910–20 revolution. Many *haciendas* were pillaged or burned down. Land reforms gave Indians the right to own land. Some huge estates remained under one ownership, particularly in Chihuahua, but many were abandoned and fell into decay.

Today, however, many of these former *haciendas* live and breathe again, converted into superb hotels in beautiful surroundings. With their lovely old rooms and graceful, arcaded, Spanish courtyards, they offer ideal accommodations for

Left and far left: the former hacienda of San Gabriel de Barrera, Guanajuato, is now a museum. Below: Hacienda del Pacifico, Ensenada

the discerning traveler with an appreciation for history.

Many *haciendas* are within range of Mexico City. The magnificent Haciendas Vista Hermosa and Cocoyoc, near Cuernavaca, have particular historical interest as former properties of the great Conquistador himself, Hernán Cortés. It doesn't take too much effort to conjure up images of famous figures of the past…

On Business

Mexico has become a member of the OECD (Organization for Economic Co-operation and Developement) and offers a wide variety of business opportunities. Despite a two-year recession, following the 1994 *peso* devaluation, there was a robust 7 percent growth in 1997, with encouraging signs of a sustained recovery.

ACCOMMODATIONS

Business executives tend to stick to centrally located hotels. The Nikko, Camino Real, Sheraton, Four Seasons, and Clarion are some of the top business hotels in Mexico City. These offer a wide range of professional services, including fax, cellular phones, secretarial, and interpreting services, and facilities for meetings and conventions. The Clarion Reforma Suites cater specially to business people.

BUSINESS ETIQUETTE

Doing business in Mexico is a very personal matter. It is important to deal directly with the top person or decision-maker, and to get on friendly terms. Meetings should start with general pleasantries before progressing gradually to hard business matters.

Entertaining plays an important role in business dealings, and working breakfasts at hotels are a popular way of mixing business with pleasure. Formal attire of suit and tie should be worn at all times in the cities.

Once back in your own country, it is important to maintain the personal contact established in Mexico. One phone call can sometimes prove far more effective than endless correspondence.

BUSINESS TRAVEL

Depending on the nature of your business, you may require a business card or visa when traveling to Mexico. Check with your local consulate. Travel within the country presents no problems, with all main centers linked by regular air services or highways. Arrangements can be made for private air transport or car rental.

COMMUNICATIONS

Mexico offers international courier services (DHL, Federal Express, and UPS), as well as local alternatives such as Estafeta and Mexpost. Phoning can still be most frustrating, although some improvements are being made. Touch-tone phones are gradually replacing old systems. Public and private faxes can be expected in most places.

CONFERENCE AND EXHIBITION FACILITIES

Major venues for large conferences and exhibitions are as follows:

Mexico City

Palacio Mundial de las Ferias, La Fragua 4. Tel: 706–63–41.
Exhibimex, Avenida Cuauhtémoc s/n, Esq Antonio M Anza. Tel: 584–18–46.
Auditorio Nacional, Paseo de la Reforma 50, Bosque de Chapultepec. Tel: 280–92–34.
Hotel Nikko, Campos Eliseos 204. Tel: 280–11–11.
Hotel Camino Real, Mariano Escobed 700. Tel: 203–21–21.
Hotel María Isabel Sheraton, Reforma 325. Tel: 207–39–33.

Acapulco
Centro Internacional Acapulco, Plaza Mexicana (tel: 84–70–50).
Acapulco Princess, Playa Revolcadero (tel: 84–31–00).

Cancún
Cancún Convention Center and Exhibition Hall, Kukulcán Boulevard, Km 9 (tel: 83–01–99).

Guadalajara
Quinta Real, Avenida México 2727, at López Mateos Sur (tel: 615–00–00).

Querétaro
Antigua Hacienda de Galindo, Carr. Amealco Km 5, off México-Querétaro highway (tel: 467–02–50).

The British Chamber of Commerce, Río de la Plata, Mexico City (tel: 256–09–01), can be of great assistance to the businessperson in providing modern office and conference facilities with equipment as required. Assistance may also be offered by the British Embassy, Commercial Affairs, Río Lerma 71, Mexico City (tel: 207–25–69).

MEDIA
The News and the *Mexico City Times* are two daily English-language newspapers which carry useful business and financial sections.

The Acapulco Convention Center, sleek and modern with all facilities

Practical Guide

ARRIVING

Travelers from the UK, Australia, New Zealand, Canada, and South Africa will need a Tourist Card, issued by airlines operating into Mexico and valid for 90 days (but can be validated for 180 days on request). A passport, valid for six months, is also required, except for Canadian and U.S. visitors who need not have passports as long as they hold proof of citizenship (birth certificate or voter registration card). A customs declaration form, presented on boarding the aircraft or at customs, must also be handed in on arrival. There are no health requirements. Visitors who require visas should always apply in their country of residence.

By air

Mexico City is well served by frequent flights from Europe, the U.S. and worldwide destinations There are also direct flights from the U.S. and Canada to other major towns and centers, with an increasing number of scheduled and chartered flights from Europe to tourist resorts such as Cancún and Puerto Vallarta.

Mexico City's airport is very busy, however, the new terminal has helped ease congestion somewhat. Taxis line up outside the airport building, and tickets are sold at special booths for a set price, according to zone. Ignore touts offering private transportation. The new circular road has greatly shortened the journey into town. For the return journey, take a taxi from your hotel, determining the price before departure.

By bus

There are first-rate bus services from the main U.S. entry points to destinations all over Mexico. Just bear in mind the distances to be covered.

By car

Travelers arriving by car must have a valid driving license, a 90-day permit for the driver of the vehicle (from Mexican Customs at the point of entry), and a fully comprehensive insurance policy (also obtainable at the border). Also carry proof of ownership of your vehicle or a letter of authorization from the owner if not traveling with you. An international driving license is also recommended for Europeans. Note that you are not permitted to leave the country without your car (on entry you will have to sign an affadavit stating that you will not sell the car in Mexico and leave photocopies of proof of ownership, driver's license, and credit card).

By rail

Rail travel is the cheapest form of transportation in Mexico, but also the slowest and often subject to delays. There are rail links with the United States at the main border towns, among which the *Aztec Eagle*, which runs from Nuevo Laredo down to Mexico City, is considered one of the better services. The *Thomas Cook Overseas Timetable*, published bi-monthly, gives details of many rail, bus, and shipping services worldwide and will help you plan a rail journey. It is available in the UK from some stations, any branch of Thomas Cook or by phoning 01733 503571/2. In the United States, contact the Forsyth Travel Library Inc, 226 Westchester Avenue, White Plains, New York 10604 (tel: (800) 367 7984 – toll-free).

CAMPING

Campsites and trailer parks are found in many parts of the country, including some of the National Parks. In some coastal areas you can rent a hammock and sleep under a *palapa* (open thatched-roof hut). Never camp overnight on the beach, or in any spot other than a designated site.

CHILDREN

On domestic flights an adult is entitled to travel with one infant (under two years of age) not occupying a seat. Children up to 12 years must pay the child's fare, usually 50–67 percent of the adult fare. On long-distance bus rides, children pay full fare if occupying a seat, while for rail travel there are usually reductions.

Many hotels have rooms for three people, or can provide an extra bed for a child. Some can also provide baby-sitting services on request. Some restaurants offer children's portions at lower prices.

CLIMATE

See page 26, and charts on page 182.

CLOTHING

Take casual, comfortable clothes for touring around, beachwear for coastal resorts, and more formal attire for Mexico City; headgear against the tropical sun; appropriate shoes for exploring cobbled streets and ruins; protection against the rain (you can get a surprise, even in the dry season); also a jacket or sweater for high altitudes. In December or January, women may need a coat at night in Mexico City (see page 26).

CONVERSION TABLES

See tables on page 183.

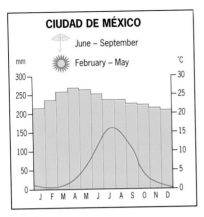

CIUDAD DE MÉXICO

June – September

February – May

WEATHER CONVERSION CHART
25.4mm = 1 inch
°F = 1.8 × °C + 32

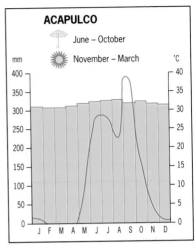

ACAPULCO

June – October

November – March

CRIME

The same principles apply in Mexico as in any other country. Watch your belongings in crowded areas, and do not leave them unattended at any time. Carry the minimum of cash and do not display it. Be extra vigilant on local transportation in Mexico City. Deposit valuables in the hotel safe. Incidents of violent attacks on tourists are not common; however, stick to central and well-lit areas for walking in the evenings. Do not park in dubious-looking areas, and never leave valuables visible inside.

CUSTOMS REGULATIONS

Visitors entering Mexico are allowed: 3 liters of wine or spirits; 400 cigarettes or 50 cigars; one movie camera and one regular camera (and up to 12 rolls of film); gifts not exceeding a total of $300 (U.S.). A completed Customs Declaration Form must be handed in to Customs and a button pushed. A red

light will signal a search, while a green light indicates you can pass through without inspection. No drugs, weapons, or pornography may be brought in, and no pre-Columbian art or artifacts may be taken out.

DISABLED TRAVELERS

Wheelchairs are available at Mexico City airport and others on request. Certain hotels have at least one room or unit accessible to wheelchair users, and some inbound tour operators, such as Grey Line Tours, can provide them on tour.

DRIVING

Car rental requirements are a valid driver's license (an International Driving License is recommended), passport, and a driver over 25. Insurance is arranged through the rental company, and payment is usually by credit card. Check car and contents thoroughly before accepting it, making sure tools and a spare tire are in place. Maximum speed limit is usually about 100km/h or as indicated, and can go down to 30km/h in some cities. Unleaded gasoline, *Magna Premio* and *Magna Sin* are now readily available. Watch out for *topes* (road bumps) and cattle. Avoid driving at night. *Angeles Verdes* (Green Angels) patrol the highways to offer free assistance at all times.

DRUGS
Trafficking in or being in possession of drugs is a federal offense, and penalties are extremely severe.

ELECTRICITY
Most of Mexico operates on 110 volts A/C, 60 cycles. From Europe, you need to bring an adaptor for 2-pin flat plugs in use here.

EMBASSIES AND CONSULATES
The following are all in Mexico City:

Australia Plaza Polanco, Torre B, Jaime Balmes 11, Colonia los Morales. Tel: 395–94–69/99–88.
Canada Schiller 529. Tel: 724–79–00.
UK Río Lerma 71. Tel: 207–20–89/ 21–49.
U.S. Reforma 305. Tel: 211–00–42.
   There are also consulates and consular representatives in other major towns.

EMERGENCY TELEPHONE NUMBERS
Ambulance, fire, police 080
Cruz Roja (Red Cross) 557–57–57 or 557–57–58
American British Cowdray Hospital (ABC), for emergencies 230–81–61.

The Thomas Cook Worldwide Customer Promise offers free emergency assistance at any Thomas Cook Network

Men's Suits

UK	36	38	40	42	44	46	48
Rest of Europe	46	48	50	52	54	56	58
US	36	38	40	42	44	46	48

Dress Sizes

UK	8	10	12	14	16	18
France	36	38	40	42	44	46
Italy	38	40	42	44	46	48
Rest of Europe	34	36	38	40	42	44
US	6	8	10	12	14	16

Men's Shirts

UK	14	14.5	15	15.5	16	16.5	17
Rest of Europe	36	37	38	39/40	41	42	43
US	14	14.5	15	15.5	16	16.5	17

Men's Shoes

UK	7	7.5	8.5	9.5	10.5	11
Rest of Europe	41	42	43	44	45	46
US	8	8.5	9.5	10.5	11.5	12

Women's Shoes

UK	4.5	5	5.5	6	6.5	7
Rest of Europe	38	38	39	39	40	41
US	6	6.5	7	7.5	8	8.5

Conversion Table

FROM	TO	MULTIPLY BY
Inches	Centimeters	2.54
Feet	Meters	0.3048
Yards	Meters	0.9144
Miles	Kilometers	1.6090
Acres	Hectares	0.4047
Gallons	Liters	4.5460
Ounces	Grams	28.35
Pounds	Grams	453.6
Pounds	Kilograms	0.4536
Tons	Tonnes	1.0160

To convert back, for example from centimeters to inches, divide by the number in the third column.

location to travelers who have purchased their travel tickets at a Thomas Cook location. The Thomas Cook travelers' check refund is a 24-hour service. Report loss or theft within 24 hours, tel: 95–800–223–7373 or 00 44 1733 318 950 (U.K. number, reverse charges).

HEALTH

Travel abroad can result in stomach problems. Strict food and water hygiene will help avoid problems with diarrhea, commonly known as *turista*. Make sure food has been properly washed and prepared; drink bottled water only.

If you are thinking of traveling inland or heading slightly off the beaten track, you should consider taking anti-malarial tablets. As in every other part of the world, AIDS is present.

HITCHHIKING

Not to be recommended, as hitch-hikers take the same risks as anywhere. Very ill advised for women on their own.

INSURANCE

Travelers to Mexico should take out fully comprehensive insurance to cover illness, loss or theft, and flight cancellation. Report any loss or theft to the police to get the necessary written confirmation for insurance claims.

LOST PROPERTY

Anything lost should be reported appropriately, as soon as possible. If lost items are returned to you, it is common courtesy to give a token reward.

MAPS

Maps tend to be expensive in Mexico and not always up to date or accurate. Pemex (the state oil company) and Guía Roji produce maps and city plans.

MEDIA

English-language newspapers include *The News* (daily), the *Mexico City Times* (daily except Sunday) and the *Daily Bulletin*, which is distributed free except on a Monday. In addition, major U.S. dailies are readily available at kiosks in Mexico City and in many resorts. *Tiempo Libre*, *Donde?* and *This Week-Esta Semana* are among any number of publications containing useful information on what to see and do.

Mexico has six private television channels, one state-owned and an extra 16 channels by satellite, in addition to cable and Multivision TV, which offer English-speaking channels. Most films are dubbed into Spanish, although satellite TV has American films shown in English. Major hotels usually have satellite and in-room cable TV, offering an assortment of Mexican and U.S. stations. Two radio stations broadcast in English. One is an FM station that transmits news bulletins; another is found on AM 590. Check with your hotel for details.

MONEY MATTERS

In 1993, the new unit of currency, called the *nuevo* (new) *peso* (**N$**), came into effect, equivalent in value to 1,000 old pesos. Coins are in denominations of 10, 20, and 50 *centavos* and 1, 2, 5, and 10 new pesos. Bills are in denominations of 10, 20, 50, 100, 200, and 500 new pesos.

U.S. dollars ($) are often accepted in Mexico, and prices can sometimes be given in dollars – not to be confused with the similar peso sign (**N$**).

All the major banks or their representatives are found in Mexico City and other main towns. If you have proper identification, you can change travelers' checks in most of the big banks and obtain cash against the major credit cards. Major credit cards that are widely accepted are American Express, Visa, MasterCard, Carte Blanche, and Diners.

Travelers' checks must be in U.S. dollars. Thomas Cook MasterCard travelers' checks free you from the hazards of carrying large amounts of cash, and in the event of loss or theft, can quickly be replaced. Many hotels, larger restaurants, and some shops in main tourist areas accept travelers' checks in lieu of cash.

The following branches of Thomas Cook can provide emergency assistance in the case of loss or theft of Thomas Cook MasterCard travelers' checks:
Banca Promex, Rio Amazonas No. 91 ler Piso, Col. Cuauhtémoc, Mexico DF (tel: 5208 003 2132).
Cia Gamesa, Poniente 116 No. 536, Col. Industrial Vallejo, Mexico DF (tel: 328 3257).
Lobby Hotel Continental Plaza Airport, Fundidora de Monterrey No. 89, Col Peñon de los Baños, Mexico City Airport (tel: 5 2300514).
Varsovia No. 44, 7 Piso, Col. Juárez, Mexico DF (tel: 5525 2675).
Circunvalación Agustín Yañez, No. 2343, Local D, Col. Moderna, Guadalajara (tel: 3 6153101/6153).

LANGUAGE

While English is quite widely spoken in tourist resorts, some knowledge of Spanish is helpful and may be quite useful when traveling off the beaten track.

Pronunciation
a as in palm
e as in late or get
i as in feet
o as in pot
u as in pull
y as in feet.

c like **s** before the letters **e** and **i**, otherwise like **k**
ch as in **ch**urch
g like **h** as in **h**at before **e** and **i**, otherwise as in **g**o
h is always silent
j like **h** in ha
ll usually like **y** in yet
ñ like **ni** in on**i**on
qu like **k**
r is rolled
s is generally as in **s**it
v tends to be like **b**
x usually as in ta**x**i, before a consonant, like **s** in **s**it, in Indian words, often like the **ch** in lo**ch**.

Numbers

0 cero	7 siete	14 catorce	30 treinta
1 uno	8 ocho	15 quince	40 cuarenta
2 dos	9 nueve	16 dieciseis	50 cincuenta
3 tres	10 diez	17 diecisiete	100 cien
4 cuatro	11 once	18 dieciocho	500 quinientos
5 cinco	12 doce	19 diecinueve	1,000 mil
6 seis	13 trece	20 veinte	10,000 diez mil

Basic phrases

good morning	buenos días
good afternoon	buenas tardes
goodnight	buenas noches
goodbye	adiós
please	por favor
many thanks	muchas gracias
you're welcome	de nada
yes	sí
no	no
Pleased to meet you	Mucho gusto
How are you?	¿Cómo está usted?
Fine, thank you	Muy bien, gracias
Do you speak English?	¿Habla usted inglés?
I don't speak Spanish	No hablo español
I don't understand	No entiendo
What is your name?	¿Cuál es su nombre?
My name is...	Yo me llamo...
Do you have...?	¿Tiene usted...?
Where is (the)...?	¿Dónde está (el/la)...?
How much is...?	¿Cuánto es...?
What time is it?	¿Qué hora es?

Directions

How can I get to...?	¿Cómo puedo llegar a...?
turn right	a la derecha
turn left	a la izquierda
straight on	derecho

Transportation

bus	el autobus
train	el tren
car	el auto
gasoline	la gasolina
parking	estacionamiento
it doesn't work	no funciona

Places

airport	el aeropuerto
bus station	la terminal de autobuses
railway station	la estación de ferrocarriles
embassy	la embajada
hospital	el hospital/la clínica
toilet	el baño
street	la calle
town	la ciudad
village	el pueblo
post office	la casa de correos
pharmacist	la farmacia
tourist office	la oficina de turismo
gas station	la gasolinera
doctor	el médico

Time

today	hoy
tomorrow	mañana
yesterday	ayer
this week	esta semana
next week	la semana que viene
now	ahora

Food

first course	entremeses
bread	pan
meat	carne
fish	pescado
pork	cerdo
chicken	pollo
lamb	cordero
veal	ternera
prawns	gambas
shrimp	camarones
salad	ensalada
ssing (oil/garlic)	al mojo de ajo
vegetables	legumbres
ice-cream	helado
fruit	fruta
cream	crema

Drinks

cocktail	un coctel
with/without ice	con/sin hielo
wine	vino
red, white, rosé	tinto, blanco, rosado
beer	cerveza
mineral water	agua mineral
sparkling water	agua con gas
coffee	café
tea	te
milk	leche

Others

breakfast	el desayuno
lunch	la comida
dinner	la cena
the bill, please	la cuenta, por favor

NATIONAL HOLIDAYS

Dates marked with an asterisk (*) are not official holidays, but people generally don't work on these days.

1 January New Year's Day
6 January Epiphany*
5 February Constitution Day
21 March Benito Juárez Day
March/April Maundy Thursday/
  Good Friday*
1 May Labor Day
5 May Battle of Puebla
1 September President's Report
16 September Independence Day
12 October Columbus Day (Day of
  the Race)
1 November All Saints' Day*
2 November Day of the Dead*
20 November Revolution Day
12 December Virgin of Guadalupe*
25 December Christmas Day

OPENING HOURS

The following is a general guide only.
Banks Monday to Friday 9am–1:30pm, extending to about 5pm in some larger cities. (Saturdays 10am–1.30pm in certain cases.)
Stores Monday to Saturday 9am–8pm, or later in resorts.
Post offices Monday to Friday 8am–6pm.
Municipal and government buildings daily 8am–8pm.
Museums Tuesday to Sunday 10am–5pm.
Churches and cathedrals daily 8am–1pm, 4–6pm.
Archaeological sites daily 8am–5pm.

ORGANIZED TOURS

A wide selection is available from most parts of Mexico. Contact the following tour operators: Cathy Matos Mexican Tours (tel: 0171 284–2550), tailor-made arrangements; Journey Latin America (tel: 0181 747–8315); and Kuoni Travel Ltd (Tel: 01306 740888); Thomson Holidays (tel: 0171 383-1330).

Local tours can be arranged on arrival. Greyline Tours (Calle Londres 166-tel: 208–11–63/13–04) offers a wide selection of tours from half-day to seven-day tours. Collection from your hotel can usually be arranged, if centrally located.

PHARMACIES

Farmacías are stocked with a good selection of drugs, medicines, and requirements for minor ailments such as nausea, throat infections, sunburn, and insect bites. Many prescription items are sold over the counter here. Opening hours are in line with other stores, and many towns have 24-hour service.

PHOTOGRAPHY

Some archaeological sites and museums may make a small charge for the use of a video camera. In certain areas, notably Chiapas, the indigenous people can object to being photographed, so respect their traditions. Bring plenty of film with you, as it is expensive in Mexico, not always of good quality, and sometimes out of date.

PLACES OF WORSHIP

Mexico is predominantly a Catholic country. Churches of other denominations are found only in larger towns. In Mexico City, details of services in English are published in *The News*.

POLICE

Tourist police, who wear square badges of red, green, and white, are around in Mexico City to help in any way possible.

Some have a knowledge of English, and you will find them friendly and willing.

POST OFFICES

Most towns have a post office, with *Poste restante* available (identification must be shown when collecting mail). Mailboxes (*buzones*) are mainly yellow with some Red Express mailboxes to be found along Reforma, and in the capital's central areas.

PUBLIC TRANSPORTATION
Air

Mexico has an extensive network of domestic air services linking all major towns and resorts. In addition to the two principal operators, Aeromexico and Mexicana, a number of regional airlines offer competitive fares, such as Taesa, Aviasca, Aereo-Caribe, and Aero California. Air travel is a popular means of transportation in Mexico, and flights are often full, so it is prudent to make advance reservations. There is an airport departure tax on international flights and some domestic. However, this is often included in the ticket, so check with your tour operator or the airline.

Bus and rail

Bus services range from top-luxury express buses with toilet, air-conditioning, soft drinks, and loud videos, to the more basic short-distance buses, which stop and pick up passengers along the roadside. All towns have one or more bus terminals, which operate very efficiently. Luggage-storage facilities are available at the larger terminals.

Trains are even cheaper than buses, but are slow and unreliable. Highly recommended, however, is the Copper Canyon ride (see pages 138–9).

Local transportation

Mexico City's metro is efficient and incredibly cheap, but not recommended during peak hours. Local buses are packed and strictly for locals. There are usually plenty of the metered green or yellow Volkswagen taxis about, and these are required by law to have the meter turned on. The larger *sitios*, which take radio calls and also stand outside hotels, charge a set price for the journey; this should always be determined beforehand. In the regions, taxis are generally plentiful. These have no meters and charge a set amount, which is usually not expensive.

STUDENT AND YOUTH TRAVEL

Students can get cheaper international flights through student travel organizations. Students with an International Student Identity Card (ISIC) can often get discounts on transportation and entry into museums and other public places, subject to local arrangements. (For youth hostels, see page 175.)

TELEPHONES

Making a telephone call in Mexico can be fraught with difficulties, requiring much patience at times. For long-distance calls, which can be costly from your hotel, try public booths (using a Ladatel phone card) or call collect (*par cobrar*) if appropriate.

Useful numbers are **090** (international operator); **020** (long-distance operator); **010** (Mexican information operator).

TIME

Most of Mexico is on Central Standard Time (6 hours behind GMT). The northwestern states of Nayarit, Sinaloa,

Sonora, and Baja California Sur operate on Mountain Time (7 hours behind GMT). Baja California Norte is on Pacific Standard Time (8 hours behind GMT).

TIPPING

Service is rarely included in restaurant bills, and a 10–15 percent tip is expected. Mexicans in the service industry, as in most countries, generally receive low wages, and it is usual to tip for any service rendered. The exception is taxis: tips are not normally expected, unless the driver has been particularly helpful in some way.

TOILETS

In major airports and good restaurants, toilets are usually of reasonable standard. In more rustic areas, they can be decidedly discouraging. It helps to carry your own soap and toilet paper.

TOURIST OFFICES

The Secretaría de Turismo (Sectur) is the official Mexican Government Ministry of Tourism. The head office in Mexico City is located at President Mazaryk 172, Polanco, with a 24-hour multilingual Hotline information service (tel: 250–01–23).

Brochures and information on Mexico City can be obtained from the Mexico City Government Tourism Bureau, at Amberes 54. Information by phone can be obtained by calling its INFOTUR service (tel: 525–93–80), also manned by multilingual operators. An additional information office is within the Fonart handicraft store at Avenida Juárez 89. All the main towns and resorts have one or more tourist offices, with a list usually obtainable from your local Mexican tourist office.

ACKNOWLEDGMENTS

The Automobile Association wishes to thank the following organizations, libraries and photographers for
their assistance in the preparation of this book.

JAMES DAVIS TRAVEL PHOTOGRAPHY spine; **A KRAUS** 138, 139, 157a, 157b, 159, 168b, 169, 176, 177a,
186; **NATURE PHOTOGRAPHERS LTD** 126/7, 126 (P R Sterry).
The remaining pictures are held in the AA Photo Library and were taken by Rick Strange with the exception
of pages 2, 5, 7b, 8, 9, 18, 21, 122/3, 124, 125a, 125b, 126, 127, 128, 129, 130, 131, 149a, 152, 154, 160,
162 and 163 which were taken by Robert Holmes; 119 and 172 which were taken by Eric Meacher and 80,
115, 116, 117, 118, 165a, 167b and 177b which were taken by Peter Wilson.

The author would like to thank the following organizations and hotels for their assistance:
Secretaría de Turismo (SECTUR), Mexico City; Mexican Tourist Office, London; Sr Carlos Velázquez Cerda,
Mexico City Government Tourism Bureau; Susan Edwards, Thomas Cook, Mexico City; Hotel Vasco de
Quiroga, Mexico City; Subsecretaría de Turismo, Guanajuato; Secretaría de Turismo, Puerto Vallarta;
Secretaría de Fomento Económico-Dirección de Turismo, Tuxtla Gutiérrez; Delegado de Turismo, San
Cristóbal de las Casas; Las Hadas Hotel, Manzanillo; Hotel Meliá Cabo Real, San José del Cabo (Baja
California Sur).

CONTRIBUTORS

Series adviser: Melissa Shales   **Copy editor:** Janet Tabinski   **Indexer:** Marie Lorimer
Thanks also to **Mona King** for her updating work on this revised edition.

displayed in traditional music and dance. Jalisco's infectious *mariachi* rhythms, Veracruz's merry *sones*, the Yucatán's romantic *trovas* and graceful dancers, the Western-style sound of *norteño* music – all present a delightfully different facet of the Mexican character.

Some of the dances survived the culture shock of the Conquest, and continue to impress today's visitors as they undoubtedly did the first Spaniards. See, if you can, the *Venado* (stag dance) from Sonora in the north; the dance of the *Viejitos* (old men) from Michoacán; the *Panachos* (feather dance) from Oaxaca; or the *Quetzales*, with striking wheel-like headdresses, from Cuetsalán, Puebla. Whatever form it takes, each artistic expression personifies its locality while contributing uniquely to Mexico's complex heritage.

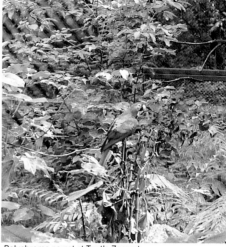
Polychrome parrot at Tuxtla Zoomat